How to Use This Book

Look for these special features in this book:

SIDEBARS, **CHARTS**, **GRAPHS**, and original **MAPS** expand your understanding of what's being discussed—and also make useful sources for classroom reports.

FAQs answer common **F**requently **A**sked **Q**uestions about people, places, and things.

WOW FACTORS offer "Who knew?" facts to keep you thinking.

TRAVEL GUIDE gives you tips on exploring the state—either in person or right from your chair!

PROJECT ROOM provides fun ideas for school assignments and incredible research projects. Plus, there's a guide to primary sources—what they are and how to cite them.

Please note: All statistics are as up-to-date as possible at the time of publication. Population data is taken from the 2010 census.

Consultants: William Loren Katz; Oscar J. Martinez, History Department, University of Arizona; Jon Spencer, Arizona Geological Survey

Book production by The Design Lab

Library of Congress Cataloging-in-Publication Data
Somervill, Barbara A.
 Arizona / by Barbara A. Somervill. — Revised edition.
 pages cm. — (America the beautiful, third series)
 Includes bibliographical references and index.
 Audience: Ages 9–12.
 ISBN 978-0-531-28275-5 (lib. bdg.)
 1. Arizona—Juvenile literature. I. Title.
 F811.3.S66 2014
 979.1—dc23   2013044319

1 2 3 4 5 6 7 8 9 10 R 24 23 22 21 20 19 18 17 16 15

America the Beautiful

Arizona

Revised Edition

BY BARBARA A. SOMERVILL

Third Series, Revised Edition

Children's Press®
An Imprint of Scholastic Inc.
New York ★ Toronto ★ London ★ Auckland ★ Sydney
Mexico City ★ New Delhi ★ Hong Kong
Danbury, Connecticut

CONTENTS

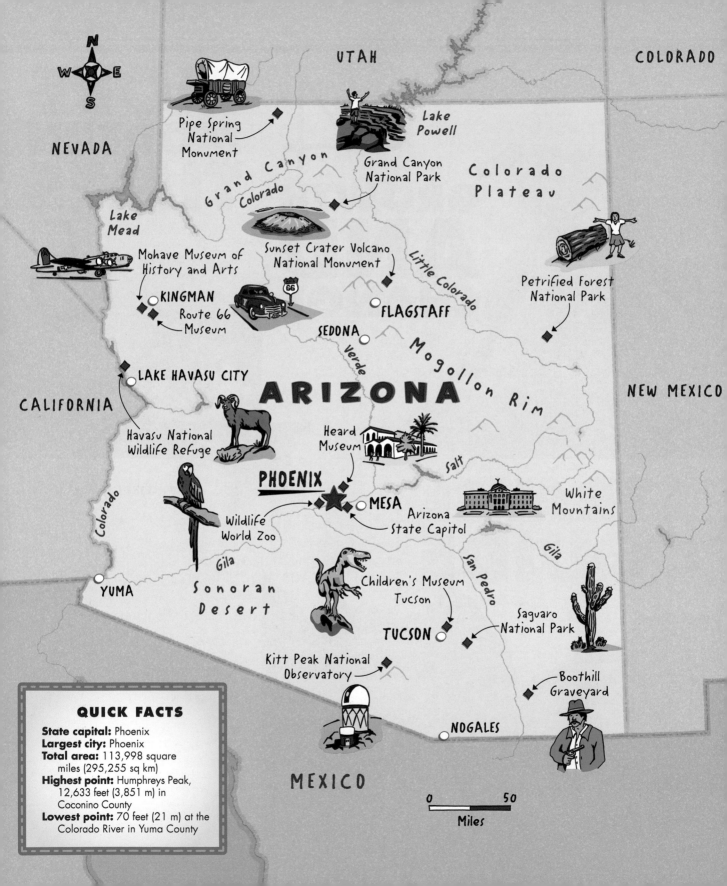

N W E S

UTAH

COLORADO

NEVADA

Pipe Spring
National
Monument

Grand Canyon

Lake
Powell

Grand Canyon
National Park

Colorado
Plateau

Lake
Mead

Colorado

Little Colorado

Mohave Museum of
History and Arts

Sunset Crater Volcano
National Monument

Petrified Forest
National Park

KINGMAN
Route 66
Museum

66

FLAGSTAFF

Mogollon Rim

SEDONA

Verde

LAKE HAVASU CITY

ARIZONA

CALIFORNIA

NEW MEXICO

Havasu National
Wildlife Refuge

Heard
Museum

Salt

Colorado

PHOENIX

Wildlife
World Zoo

MESA

Arizona
State Capitol

White
Mountains

Gila

Gila

YUMA

Sonoran
Desert

Children's Museum
Tucson

San Pedro

Saguaro
National Park

TUCSON

Kitt Peak National
Observatory

Boothill
Graveyard

NOGALES

MEXICO

QUICK FACTS

State capital: Phoenix
Largest city: Phoenix
Total area: 113,998 square
miles (295,255 sq km)
Highest point: Humphreys Peak,
12,633 feet (3,851 m) in
Coconino County
Lowest point: 70 feet (21 m) at the
Colorado River in Yuma County

0   50
Miles

Welcome to Arizona!

HOW DID ARIZONA GET ITS NAME?

No one is sure where the name *Arizona* came from, but historians have several ideas. It may have evolved from *aleh-zon* or *ali-shonak*, which mean "small spring" or "place of the small spring" in the language of the Pima people. Their traditional lands lie in what are now southern Arizona and northern Mexico. Other sources trace the name to Juan Bautista de Anza, a Spanish explorer. He came from the Basque region of Spain, and *arizona* is a Basque word for "good oak tree." Regardless of which version is true, Arizona has had its name for at least 300 years.

TEXAS

8

READ ABOUT

Arizona's landscape offers many spectacular opportunities for mountain bikers and other adventurers.

CHAPTER ONE

LAND

★

ARIZONA IS A LAND OF DRAMATIC AND DIVERSE SCENERY. Locals and tourists alike marvel at its soaring mountains, red-walled canyons, crumbling cliffs, vast deserts, and oddly shaped rock formations. Arizona spreads across 113,998 square miles (295,255 square kilometers) of land. Humphreys Peak, at 12,633 feet (3,851 meters), is Arizona's highest point. The lowest point is only 70 feet (21 m) above sea level at the Colorado River.

A cross-country skier cuts through a ponderosa pine forest in Fay Canyon.

Arizona Geo-Facts

Along with the state's geographical highlights, this chart ranks Arizona's land, water, and total area compared to all other states.

Total area; rank	113,998 square miles (295,255 sq km); 6th
Land; rank	113,635 square miles (294,315 sq km); 6th
Water; rank	364 square miles (943 sq km); 48th
Inland water; rank	364 square miles (943 sq km); 42nd
Geographic center	Yavapai County, 55 miles (89 km) east to southeast of Prescott
Latitude	31°20' N to 37° N
Longitude	109°3' W to 114°50' W
Highest point	Humphreys Peak, 12,633 feet (3,851 m) in Coconino County
Lowest point	70 feet (21 m) at the Colorado River in Yuma County
Largest city	Phoenix
Longest river	Colorado

Source: U.S. Census Bureau, 2010 census

Arizona is the sixth-largest state. Rhode Island, the smallest state, could fit inside it 73 times.

FINDING ARIZONA

Arizona is a land of extremes. In some places, it is dry-as-a-bone desert; in other parts of the state, dense forests cover the land. In summer, the temperatures soar to well over 100 degrees Fahrenheit (38 degrees Celsius), while winter can bring chilling winds and snow to some places. Arizona shares its borders with New Mexico to the east, Utah to the north, and Nevada and California to the west. The country of Mexico lies along Arizona's southern border.

LAND REGIONS

Despite its size, Arizona has only two major land regions, the Colorado **Plateau** and the Basin and Range.

The Colorado Plateau

The Colorado Plateau is a huge, uplifted landmass that covers northern Arizona. The plateau extends across the Four Corners region of northeastern Arizona well into Utah, Colorado, and northwestern New Mexico. Over millions of years, rivers have carved deep into the land, forming gorges, ravines, and canyons. The Colorado River, now tamed by dams, flows through this region. The ancient Colorado sliced through the red ribbons of plateau stone to form the Grand Canyon. This majestic canyon features stark cliffs and crumbling slopes, all in beautiful, muted colors.

The Colorado River flows through the Grand Canyon.

WORD TO KNOW

plateau *an elevated part of the earth with steep slopes*

FAQ

Q: **WHAT ARE THE FOUR CORNERS?**

A: This is the only spot in the United States where four state borders meet. Many visitors stand on the intersection of the Arizona, Utah, Colorado, and New Mexico borders so they can claim they are in all four states at the same time.

Arizona Topography

Use the color-coded elevation chart to see on the map Arizona's high points (dark red to orange) and low points (green to dark green). Elevation is measured as the distance above or below sea level.

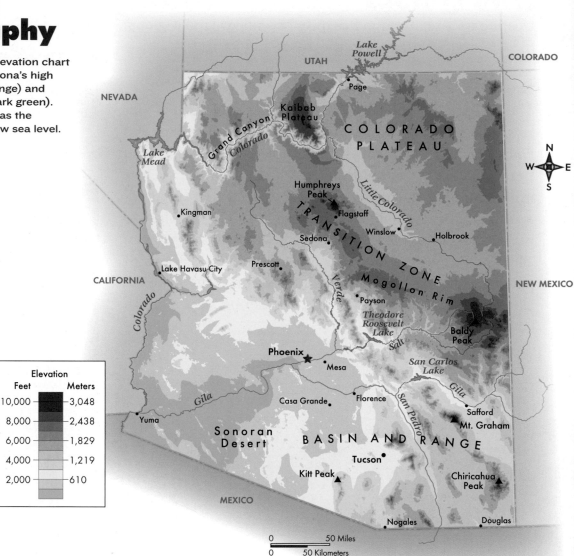

Elevation	
Feet	Meters
10,000	3,048
8,000	2,438
6,000	1,829
4,000	1,219
2,000	610

The plateau region includes mountain ranges such as the White Mountains and the San Francisco Peaks. Many volcanoes once shook this region. Sugarloaf Mountain and Eldon Mountain are domes formed by bulges of melted rock underground. Humphreys Peak, the state's tallest mountain, is actually an eroded volcano that has not erupted for many thousands of years. Sunset Crater, which is more than 1,000 feet (305 m) high, last erupted about 900 years ago.

The Basin and Range

The Basin and Range region features small mountain ranges alternating with desert. Ranges such as the Chiricahuas, Huachucas, and Dragoons rise in the middle of the sprawling Arizona desert. These ranges were formed not by volcanoes but by earthquake faults folding and tilting the earth's crust. These smaller mountain chains are like cool islands in the midst of the desert. They provide variety to the landscape and are a welcome home for a host of animals and a wide range of spruces and firs.

Most of Arizona is desert. The Painted Desert in west-central Arizona is stunning. At sunset, reds, golds, and browns form a beautiful picture.

Three deserts spread across the southern part of the state. The Mojave Desert juts into Arizona from California. Some of the land is pockmarked with playas—temporary lakes—that fill after winter rainstorms. Few cacti grow in the Mojave.

Two-thirds of the Chihuahuan Desert lies in Mexico, but parts of it reach into southeastern Arizona. This region endures extremely hot summers, chilly winters, and dramatic thunderstorms. Most of its 8 inches (20 centimeters) of annual rainfall comes in the summer. This is a shrub desert, where yucca, agave, and creosote cover most of the land. Javelinas—wild pigs—use their razor-sharp tusks to feed on their favorite food, prickly pear cactus. Mule

SEE IT HERE!

PETRIFIED FOREST NATIONAL PARK

The Painted Desert is part of the Petrified Forest National Park. More than 225 million years ago, this region was covered by forest. Eventually, the trees died and fell to the ground. Water carrying minerals washed over and through the logs. The logs gradually filled with minerals, until they turned into colorful stone. Visitors can now walk among the beautiful stone logs.

A young javelina

The Gila monster is the only venomous lizard in the United States.

Q8 WHY DO MORE CACTI GROW IN THE SONORAN AND CHIHUAHUAN DESERTS THAN IN THE MOJAVE?

A8 Cacti have broad, shallow roots that absorb water effectively after brief, heavy summer rains that may not soak very far into the soil. The Sonoran and Chihuahuan deserts receive these summer rains, but the Mojave receives most of its rainfall in the winter.

Ironwoods have the heaviest wood of any living tree. The wood from an ironwood weighs about 66 pounds (30 kilograms) per cubic foot (0.028 cubic m). White pine, by comparison, weighs only 26 pounds (12 kg) per cubic foot.

deer browse on low-lying plants. At night, a coyote's howl may be answered by the braying of wild burros.

The Sonoran Desert sweeps across more than 100,000 square miles (259,000 sq km) of southern Arizona and northern Mexico. It is a very hot, very dry desert, but it is full of life. Stands of ironwood trees thrive on the desert floor. On the slopes at the base of mountains and near water sources, mesquite, ash, black walnut, and cottonwood survive in the desert heat. Dozens of kinds of cacti dot the landscape, but none is more imposing than the saguaro, which can grow to 75 feet (23 m) tall. Rattlesnakes and Gila monsters find empty rocks for sunning themselves in the hot afternoon. Kit foxes, kangaroo rats, ground squirrels, and jackrabbits nibble on grasses at dawn before burrowing into their dens for a long day's sleep. Gila woodpeckers poke holes in the sides of cacti, only to have their holes occupied by small elf owls or cactus wrens.

RIVERS AND LAKES

The Colorado is Arizona's longest river. It begins in the Rocky Mountains of Colorado, cuts across northern Arizona, and then forms the state's western border before flowing into the Gulf of California in Mexico. Other major rivers in the state are the Gila, the Salt, the Verde, and the Bill Williams. Much of Arizona is so dry that small creeks and streams are sometimes listed as rivers. In fact, some rivers are "dry" rivers. They are riverbeds that carry water only after major rains or in the early spring when mountain snows melt.

The state's major rivers have been dammed to create lakes that provide water for drinking and irrigation. The Glen Canyon Dam in northern Arizona holds back the Colorado, forming Lake Powell, the state's largest lake. These dams have left some rivers with little water in them. The Gila River flows into the Colorado near Yuma, in the

The Glen Canyon Dam holds back the Colorado River to form Lake Powell.

southwest corner of the state. Today, irrigation and damming have reduced the natural flow of the Gila to a trickle.

CLIMATE

Arizonans often boast that their state has a dry heat, making it more comfortable than places where there is a lot of moisture in the air. Still, there's no question that Arizona is hot. The average daily high temperatures for June, July, and August rise above 90°F (32°C). Winter brings mild temperatures to the desert, with high temperatures of about 70°F (21°C). At night, the temperature can drop below freezing.

Weather Report

This chart shows record temperatures (high and low) for the state, as well as average temperatures (July and January) and average annual precipitation for Arizona.

Record high temperature . . . . 128°F (53°C) at Lake Havasu on June 29, 1994

Record low temperature . . . . –40°F (–40°C) at Hawley Lake near McNary on January 7, 1971

Average July temperature, Phoenix . . . . .95°F (35°C)

Average January temperature, Phoenix . . . . .56°F (13°C)

Average yearly precipitation, Phoenix . . . . . .8 inches (20 cm)

Source: National Climatic Data Center, NESDIS, NOAA, U.S. Department of Commerce

WORD TO KNOW

precipitation *all water that falls to the earth, including rain, sleet, hail, snow, dew, fog, and mist*

Most **precipitation** in Arizona comes in the form of rainfall. Heavy thunderstorms are common in southern Arizona in July and August. From November through March, storm systems from the Pacific Ocean often cross the state. These winter storms bring rain and sometimes heavy snow to the mountains in the central and northern areas. Northern Arizona receives much more precipitation than the south. Flagstaff may have 70 days a year of measurable rainfall, while Yuma has rain only 15 days a year.

High winds blow both rain and dust across the state. It all begins in spring with hot, dry winds. The wind kicks up dust, creating dust devils and dust storms. Dust devils are like tornadoes with a funnel of dust and dirt. Dust storms are called haboobs. The word *haboob* comes from the Arabic word for wind. In August 2013, one haboob knocked over trees and left 14,000 Arizona residents without electricity.

As the air warms, it begins to carry more moisture, which turns into heavy but brief rains that Arizonans call monsoons. Because the land is so dry, rainwater cannot soak in. Instead, it runs across the land as dangerous flash floods.

PLANT LIFE

Plants that can thrive with limited water find Arizona ideal. More than 3,370 plant species are found in Arizona's mountains and deserts. The dry environment is particularly good for members of the cactus family. However, a

A variety of cacti and Mexican golden poppies at Organ Pipe Cactus National Monument

number of shrubs, trees, and grasses also do well. After a wet winter, Arizona has an incredible number of wildflowers that sprinkle color across the landscape.

The classic cactus species shown in every Western movie is the saguaro. These slow-growing cacti can take 25 years to grow just 2 feet (61 cm). They do not start getting branches until they reach about the age of 75, and some live to be more than 200 years old. The saguaro produces fruit that is heavy with seeds.

Like saguaros, prickly pear cacti produce edible fruit. Prickly pear grows close to the ground. It has branches that look like paddles with sharp needles. Its sunny yellow blossoms produce sweet fruit with lots of liquid. Barrel cactus looks like its name—a barrel. Fishhook cactus has curved, barbed spines like fishhooks. Organ pipe cactus looks much like a spider lying on its back.

One saguaro fruit can have more than 4,000 seeds.

Indian paintbrush and pinecones from
the South Rim of the Grand Canyon

The cereus is a dull, green-gray cactus for 364 days each year. But for one night each summer, the cereus blooms. By morning, the bloom is dead, and another will not appear until the next year.

Areas covered with shrubs may have creosote bushes, tussock grasses, or tumbleweeds. Hikers need to watch where they walk. If the spines of a cactus do not jab them, they might be caught by a catclaw acacia tree. The deserts also support a few taller plants. Joshua trees grow in the Mojave Desert. Joshua trees are members of the yucca family and grow as tall as 40 feet (12 m).

From February through May, Arizona's desert dons a wardrobe of color. Claret cup cactus has deep red flowers, while saguaros produce creamy white blossoms. Brilliant orange poppies, blue columbines, yellow sunflowers, and purple asters fill out the wildflower rainbow. Many desert blossoms carry interesting names—nodding bluebells, pink shooting stars, yellow and red monkeyflowers, and Indian paintbrush. Plants that flower at night tend to produce white flowers, which attract bats.

In parts of Arizona with a little more rain, scrub brush, grasslands, and stands of juniper, piñon, and oak grow. At higher elevations, pine trees, blue spruces, and quaking aspens thrive. And on Arizona's mountain peaks are krummholz—gnarled, stunted trees bent by high winds.

ANIMAL LIFE

Arizona is alive with animals. There are 134 species of mammals, around 550 types of birds, and more than 100 species of reptiles. As for the insect world, thousands of members of that community creep, crawl, and flitter around Arizona. The largest animals are mammals. Among the predators are coyotes, Mexican gray wolves, and mountain lions. Black bears, which live in Arizona's woodlands, eat both plants and animals. Other large plant eaters include deer, elk, bighorn sheep, mule deer, and pronghorn, a type of antelope.

Arizona's forested mountainsides are home to many smaller creatures such as chipmunks, squirrels, jackrabbits, skunks, and foxes. And on the tops of the mountains, pika, ptarmigan, and other critters thrive despite cold winters.

Antelope jackrabbit

Many bighorn sheep make their home in the Arizona wilderness.

SEE IT HERE!

WILDLIFE WORLD ZOO

Check out animals from all over the world at the Wildlife World Zoo in Litchfield Park. You'll see exotic and endangered animals, including cranes, tigers, parrots and even an all-white (albino) alligator. You'll learn how the zoo promotes wildlife conservation and find out what you can do to help.

Without question, water plays an important role in the lives of Arizona's animals. The lack of water means that animals have adapted to their environment in different ways. Some, like the desert tortoise and kangaroo rat, get nearly all their water from the plants they eat. Others, like the Gila monster, spend most of their lives underground. Coyotes, wolves, and owls hunt their prey during the night. These behaviors allow animals to survive the sweltering heat of Arizona's summers.

Some birds make their homes in Arizona throughout the year. Other birds use the state as a rest stop on their way to their winter or summer homes. The largest of the state's bird species is the California condor. With a wingspan of 10 feet (3 m), the condor soars high above the earth, using its excellent vision to search for the dead animals it eats.

On the small end, tiny elf owls and cactus wrens nestle in holes in the side of saguaro cacti. Arizona's many wildflowers attract 18 species of hummingbirds. Sulphur-bellied flycatchers and red-faced warblers join ruby-throated and Anna's hummingbirds as they flit from blossom to blossom.

A number of birds make their homes on the ground. Gambel's quail and ring-necked pheasants are common ground-dwelling birds. Roadrunners speed through the brush in search of insects. Burrowing owls find empty ground squirrel or ferret nests and move in. Meanwhile, herons and bitterns dip their bills to feed in the state's lakes and other waters.

Anna's hummingbird

Arizona National Park Areas

This map shows some of Arizona's national parks, monuments, preserves, and other areas protected by the National Park Service.

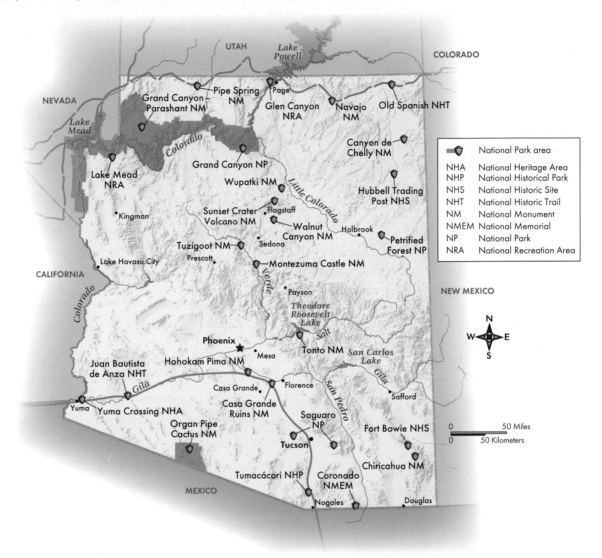

Desert areas feature a host of fascinating creatures. Arizona is home to many kinds of scorpions, along with the vinegaroon, a gruesome-looking critter that resembles the scorpion. Vinegaroons can squirt a vinegar-like spray to protect themselves. Beetles also thrive in the

THE ENDANGERED WOLF

Once, Mexican gray wolves ran wild through the mountains and deserts of the southwestern United States and northern Mexico. In 1976, the species was officially declared endangered. By 1998, only 175 Mexican gray wolves survived. That year, 11 Mexican gray wolves that had been raised in captivity were released into the wild in the Blue Range Wolf Recovery Area in eastern Arizona. In 2002, the first wild-born wolf pup litter was born to a wild-born parent—a sign that Mexican gray wolves' survival is possible in the wild. As of 2012, there were around 75 Mexican gray wolves living in the wild, with around 300 more in captivity.

This Mexican gray wolf is protected at the zoo that is part of the Arizona-Sonora Desert Museum.

Mojave rattlesnake

desert. One of the most amazing is the Hercules beetle, which can grow more than 6 inches (15 cm) long and lift hundreds of times its own weight.

Eleven species of rattlesnakes slither through the Arizona wilds. They sun themselves on rocks in the day and prefer to stay away from humans. Rattlers are venomous, but they seldom waste their poison on humans. Instead, they use it to kill prey such as rodents, lizards, and ground birds.

PROTECTING THE ENVIRONMENT

Arizona has 39 endangered and threatened animal species, and 17 endangered and threatened plants. Both plants and animals suffer from the same problems. As more people move into Arizona, humans compete with animals for habitat. Humans use water to irrigate their crops, sprinkle their lawns, and drink. Humans build dams to control the flow of rivers and recycle water through sewage treatment plants. While dams may suit humans, dams change the flow of water in rivers and alter nearby habitats.

The state's deserts have become tourist attractions, but tourists can easily damage the desert landscape by stepping on plants and crushing the soil. Plants such as Navajo sedge and Arizona agave struggle to survive in today's deserts. Cactus pygmy-owls and Mexican spotted owls are in danger of becoming extinct. Jaguars and ocelots—members of the cat family—still prowl the night desert, but for how long? They, too, have lost habitat, and their prey has become scarce.

The desert can be easily damaged. One key element in preserving desert **ecosystems** is education. Many people do not realize that riding off-road vehicles through the desert can destroy plants and animals by damaging animal burrows, crushing plants, and polluting the air. An hour of off-road fun can damage the ecosystem so badly that the desert may take years to recover. The Arizona government and **conservation** groups are working to educate Arizonans and visitors alike so that the delicate desert will be preserved for future generations to enjoy.

MINI-BIO

BRUCE BABBITT: PRESERVING THE WILDERNESS

Bruce Babbitt (1938–) was born in California but has played an important role for Arizona. He served as Arizona governor (1978–1987) and the U.S. Secretary of the Interior (1993–2001). Babbitt created in 2000 a National Landscape Conservation System that covers 27 million acres (11 million hectares) of public land. He has worked tirelessly to keep America's wilderness regions "healthy, open, and wild." He proposes that the nation identify and protect landscapes and ecosystems in the same way it protects species.

? **Want to know more?** Visit www.factsfornow.scholastic.com and enter the keyword **Arizona**.

WORDS TO KNOW

ecosystems *communities of plants and animals interacting with their environments*

conservation *the act of saving or preserving something, such as a natural resource, plant, or animal species*

READ ABOUT

Early Arizonans hunted saber-toothed tigers and other game animals.

Hohokam pottery

10,000 BCE

People arrive in what is now Arizona

▲ 100 BCE–500 CE

Mogollon, Hohokam, and Ancestral Pueblo cultures emerge

600

Hohokams begin making canals

CHAPTER TWO

FIRST PEOPLE

★

SOME SCHOLARS ESTIMATE THAT HUMANS ARRIVED IN TODAY'S ARIZONA ABOUT 12,000 YEARS AGO. At the time, a major ice age was ending, so the climate was cooler. Much of the area that is now desert was covered by forests then. Large animals such as woolly mammoths, giant sloths, and camels roamed fields and forests. There were also saber-toothed tigers, short-faced bears, and dire wolves—relatives of today's gray wolf.

700
Ancestral Pueblos begin carving cliff dwellings

1250
Arizona's early cultures begin to disappear

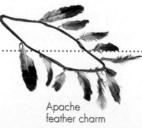
Apache feather charm

◄ **1250–1450**
Navajos and Apaches migrate to Arizona

Early hunters killed mammoths for food.

THE FIRST ARIZONANS

Early Arizonans were hunter-gatherers. Groups of people worked together to provide food. With stone-tipped spears at the ready, hunters stalked prey. They forced animals over cliffs or trapped them in canyons and then killed them with their spears. Then they butchered the meat using stone knives. Women scraped fat and gristle from the animal skins and made clothing from the skins. Women and children also gathered nuts, berries, roots, and fruit. When hunting reduced animal populations in one region, people moved to new hunting grounds.

Ten thousand years later, people still hunted and gathered their food. But as the climate warmed, the huge game animals disappeared. People began to hunt smaller mammals and fish. Between roughly 100 BCE and 500 CE, three cultures emerged in the region: Mogollon, Hohokam, and Ancestral Pueblo.

Native American Peoples

(Before European Contact)

This map shows the general area of Native American peoples before European settlers arrived.

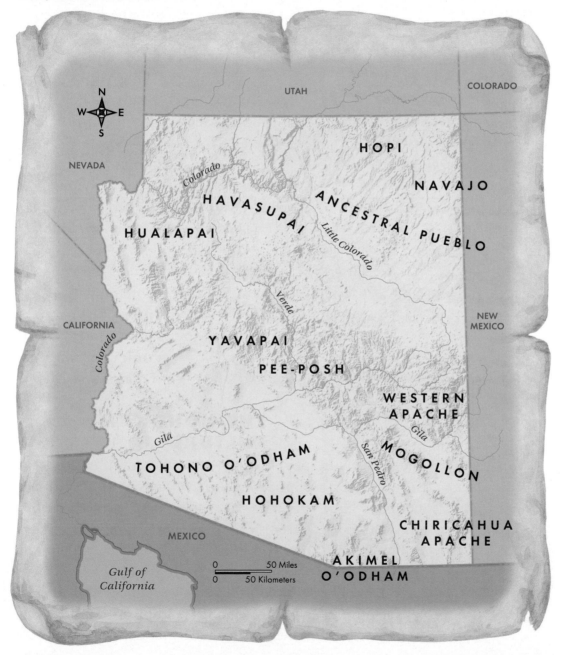

HOPI

NAVAJO

ANCESTRAL PUEBLO

HAVASUPAI

HUALAPAI

YAVAPAI

PEE-POSH

WESTERN APACHE

MOGOLLON

TOHONO O'ODHAM

HOHOKAM

CHIRICAHUA APACHE

AKIMEL O'ODHAM

UTAH

COLORADO

NEVADA

CALIFORNIA

NEW MEXICO

MEXICO

Colorado

Little Colorado

Verde

Gila

San Pedro

Gila

Gulf of California

0   50 Miles

0   50 Kilometers

EMIL HAURY: UNCOVERING HISTORY

Much of what we know about the Mogollon and Hohokam cultures comes from the work of Emil Haury (1904–1992). Haury studied **archaeology** at the University of Arizona, graduated in 1927, and returned a decade later to serve as the head of the school's archaeology department. His interests covered both human cultures and the immense beasts hunted by early Arizonans. Through his work, Haury established how the Mogollon people differed from Hohokams and Ancestral Pueblos. He also produced a timeline for the development of the Mogollon culture. His work had a lasting influence on the field of archaeology and knowledge about Arizona's ancient cultures.

? Want to know more? Visit www.factsfornow .scholastic.com and enter the keyword **Arizona**.

WORDS TO KNOW

archaeology *the study of the remains of past human societies*

geometric *using straight lines and simple shapes, such as circles or squares*

THE MOGOLLON CULTURE

The Mogollon people lived in the southeastern corner of Arizona, near what is now the border with New Mexico and Mexico. Most likely, they were the region's first farmers. They grew corn, squash, and beans. They also hunted deer, rabbits, and other wild game. Mogollons built deep pithouses—dwellings dug into the ground—that usually included a large chamber called a kiva that was used for religious ceremonies.

The Mogollon people painted or carved pictures on stone. Their potters also painted pictures on their pottery and jars. The pictures depicted mythical characters, animals, birds, **geometric** patterns, and symbols for gods.

THE HOHOKAM CULTURE

The Hohokam people may have been influenced by cultures from Central America. They built platform mounds—large mounds of earth with structures on top—and ball courts, which are commonly found in early Central American societies. More than 200 such ball courts have been found in Hohokam lands. The early Hohokam people built villages along the Salt and Gila rivers. They lived in shallow pithouses dug into the ground and strengthened by sticks and dried mud.

Like the Mogollon people, Hohokams were farmers who grew corn, beans, and squash. Many Native peoples in North America grew these crops, but Hohokams had to deal with an unusually extreme environment. In 600 CE, they began making canals to nourish the desert's dry soil. Hohokams also grew wild plants such as agave, and they made pottery that was used to cook and store food.

The Hohokam people believed in several gods. They believed that the people who had been created along with the earth died when the gods sent a great flood over the land. Siuuhu, a god formed in the "second creation," was the first to emerge from his house after the flood and became the primary god. Coyote and the Earth Doctor became lesser gods. According to Hohokam beliefs, Siuuhu guided the people to dig canals and irrigate their crops. As part of their religion, Hohokams cremated their dead. The ashes were sometimes placed in a pottery jar and buried in a small pit.

FAQ

Q8 HOW DID HOHOKAMS USE THEIR BALL COURTS?

A8 Historians believe that Hohokams played games using a heavy rubber ball. The object was probably to keep the ball in play with either the hands or feet. The movement of the ball and players on the court may have represented the movement of the sun, moon, and planets. Ball games allowed friends and neighbors from other villages to get together to discuss trade, settle problems, and arrange marriages.

The Hohokam canal system covered 500 miles (805 km) of desert and may have supported 50,000 people. Many of today's canals along the Salt and Gila rivers follow those same paths.

Hohokams playing an active ball game while others watch

This painting by Robert Wesley Amick depicts a Pueblo man near his desert village.

THE ANCESTRAL PUEBLO CULTURE

The Ancestral Pueblo people, once called Anasazi, are the ancestors of today's Hopi people. The early Pueblo people lived in pithouses, much like Hohokams and Mogollons. They established villages in the Four Corners area of northeastern Arizona. The villages included dwellings, kivas for religious ceremonies, and storage buildings. By 700, Ancestral Pueblos had begun carving dwellings into the sides of soft cliffs. These eventually developed into cliff-side cities. Many Ancestral Pueblo cliff dwellings remain today.

Historians believe that each Pueblo community had its own special skills. Some carved elegant buildings in stone cliffs, while others produced fine cotton cloth, wove baskets, or fired (baked) pottery. Villages worked together to grow, harvest, and store food. Ancestral Pueblos raised turkeys and farmed beans, corn, and squash. They stored dried corn and beans to eat when food was scarce. Men spent much of their time hunting, while women gathered wood for fires.

Religion played an important role in the lives of the Ancestral Pueblo people. People had faith in a Great Spirit, or Creator. Many religious events centered on food and water. The people prayed for rainfall, good harvests, and success in hunting.

DROUGHT AND DISEASE

Between 1250 and 1450, the early cultures of Arizona began to disappear. No one is quite sure why. According to one theory, a long drought left the people unable to grow enough food to feed themselves, and many died of starvation or disease. Scientists have studied the bones of Ancestral Pueblos from that time. Studies show that the people were poorly nourished.

Another theory is that a drought led to battles over water, in which many of the men were killed. And some people believe that the drought caused groups to raid each other for food, and that these raids grew into warfare.

Although the Ancestral Pueblo culture ended, the people did not disappear. Historians believe that their culture evolved into the Hopi culture of northeastern Arizona and the Pueblo cultures of New Mexico.

THE HOPI CULTURE

Like their ancestors, the Hopi people made pottery and farmed the land. Children inherited their family fields through their mother's side of the family.

The Hopi people believe that powerful spirits affect human life. These spirits, called kachinas, take on three forms: unseen spirits, dancers filled with the spirit, or

SEE IT HERE!

CANYON DE CHELLY

The Canyon de Chelly National Monument, one of the longest continuously inhabited locations in North America, is a blend of ancient and modern. At one time, Ancestral Pueblo people carved homes and kivas into the canyon walls. Today, members of the Navajo Nation live in the canyon. Visitors to Canyon de Chelly can explore ruins of Pueblo dwellings built between 350 and 1300 CE. They can also see drawings on cliff walls that record the history and beliefs of the people who made their life in this Arizona canyon.

Hopi kachina doll

MINI-BIO

NAMPEYO: THE BLIND POTTER

Nampeyo (1860–1942) was the first Native Arizonan potter to gain wide recognition. She was an artist, an innovator of shapes and designs, and a representative of the Hopi people. Nampeyo learned her pottery skills from her grandmother. Art collectors became interested in her work when she was still a young woman. In 1898, Nampeyo went to Chicago to demonstrate her artistry at an exhibition. She had begun losing her sight by 1925, but she did not abandon her craft. She continued to experiment and innovate. Today, her work is displayed in many museums.

❓ **Want to know more?** Visit www.factsfornow.scholastic.com and enter the keyword **Arizona**.

The Navajo Nation has the largest reservation in the United States, covering more than 27,000 square miles (70,000 sq km) of land in Arizona, New Mexico, and Utah.

WORD TO KNOW

reservation *land set aside for Native Americans to live on*

wooden statues that represent the spirit. Kachina dancers are always men, even if the spirit being represented is female.

NAVAJOS AND APACHES

Sometime between 1250 and 1450, people began to migrate southward from what is now western Canada. By 1450, several bands of people had settled in Arizona. They formed two separate groups: Navajos and Apaches.

Navajos saw how Pueblo people lived and they modeled their lifestyle on Pueblo ways. They farmed corn, beans, melons, and squash, and they wove blankets and cloth. The Navajo people lived in homes called hogans, which were made from wooden poles, tree bark, and dried mud. The doors of hogans always faced east so that people could greet the rising sun each day.

Navajos call themselves *Diné*, or "the people." Traditionally, the Diné worshipped an all-powerful god symbolized by the sun. They believed that the spirits of the dead move to another part of the universe where they carry on daily activities just as they did in their past lives.

Traditional Navajo religion uses chants to cure problems and bring good fortune. One of the central ceremonies is the Blessingway, which is used to bring health, good luck, and blessings for all.

When Apaches first arrived in Arizona, they wore clothes made of deerskin. Men wore shirts, leggings, and moccasins. Women wore shirts, skirts, and moccasins. Apaches formed six different groups—the Chiricahua, Mescalero, Jicarilla, Western Apache, Lipan, and Kiowa—that lived in the region.

Apache religious ceremonies celebrate events connected to everyday life. People pray for rain, give thanks for good crops, and recognize the beginning of adulthood. Apaches believe their spirits dwell in a land of peace and plenty, without disease or death.

Other Native American groups also lived in what would become Arizona. The Tohono O'odham and Akimel O'odham (also called Pima) peoples lived in the desert. The Yavapais, Havasupais, and Hualapais lived in the area of the Grand Canyon. Soon a new people would arrive in the Southwest. They would change forever the lives of the Native people of Arizona.

Picture Yourself . . .

in the Blessingway
You are going on a journey, and your family chants the Blessingway on your behalf. On the first night, songs are sung. In the morning, you bathe in suds from a yucca plant, as songs and prayers are said for you. Later, dry paintings are made from cornmeal and crushed flower petals, and singing lasts all through the night. At the end of the ceremony, you ask the spirits to help you and guide you on a safe path.

This Pima woman, shown with her son, is weaving a basket from yucca plants.

READ ABOUT

Estevanico exploring
the American
Southwest

1539

*Estevanico becomes
the first non-Native
person to enter
today's Arizona*

1540 ▶

*Francisco Vásquez
de Coronado crosses
Arizona on his quest
for gold*

1582

*Antonio de Espejo
discovers silver in
Arizona*

CHAPTER THREE

EXPLORATION AND SETTLEMENT

★

GOLD! The Spanish plundered Mexico for it, and many believed the legends that cities of gold existed north of present-day Mexico. In 1539, a party of Spanish fortune hunters headed north from Mexico City. The Spaniards also hoped to spread their Roman Catholic religion and create settlements in this land. An African named Estevanico served as the advance scout for the party and was the first non-Native person to set foot in Arizona.

1680
The Hopi and Pueblo peoples rebel against Spanish rule

◄**1687**
Eusebio Kino begins founding missions in Arizona

1751
Pimas revolt against Spanish rule

European Exploration of Arizona

The colored arrows on this map show the routes taken by explorers between 1539 and 1598.

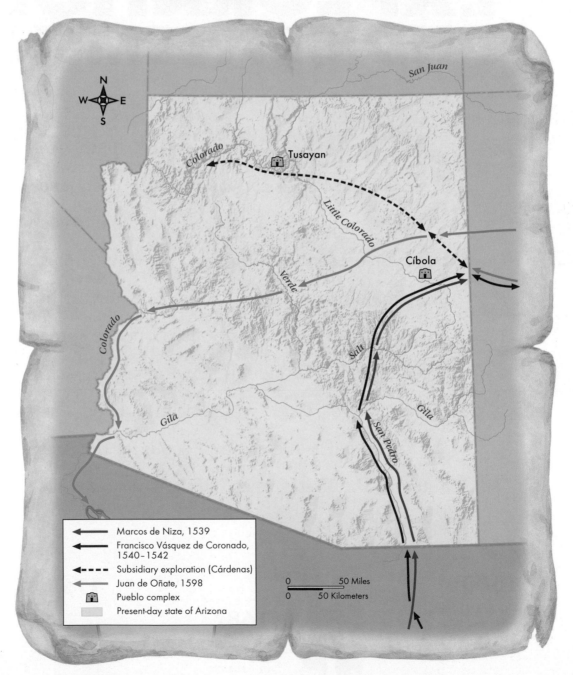

Marcos de Niza, 1539

Francisco Vásquez de Coronado, 1540–1542

Subsidiary exploration (Cárdenas)

Juan de Oñate, 1598

Pueblo complex

Present-day state of Arizona

0   50 Miles

0   50 Kilometers

TALES OF CÍBOLA

Estevanico had been enslaved by Spaniards and brought to New Spain, which is what Mexico was then called. During a gold-hunting **expedition** in 1528, he and a Spanish crew were shipwrecked near what is now Galveston, Texas. He and three Spaniards wandered through the Southwest for years trying to reach Mexico City. During that time, Estevanico learned Native American languages and heard many tales of Cíbola, the legendary Seven Cities of Gold, which the Native people told him lay north of Mexico.

Estevanico and the Spaniards finally reached Mexico City in 1536. Thrilled by Estevanico's tales of Cíbola's gold, Don Antonio de Mendoza, the governor of New Spain, ordered a priest named Marcos de Niza to lead an expedition north the following year. Estevanico and his Native American guides headed out first. They crossed the

This painting shows the Pueblo of Acoma, in neighboring New Mexico, thought to be part of Cíbola.

WORD TO KNOW

expedition *a trip for the purpose of exploration*

The city of Tucson, Arizona, named a park after Estevanico. It was the first park in the United States to be named for an African.

WORD TO KNOW

conquistadores *ones who conquer; specifically, leaders in the Spanish conquest of the Americas*

Francisco Vásquez de Coronado and his men exploring the lands north of Mexico

deserts of Mexico, through today's eastern Arizona, and into New Mexico. There Estevanico was killed by Native people. After hearing of his scout's death, de Niza continued north for a time, before turning around and heading back to Mexico City. He falsely reported that he had found the Seven Cities of Gold. This report stirred New Spain's rulers to send further explorations.

TRAVELING WITH CORONADO

In 1540, Francisco Vásquez de Coronado was a Spanish official in Mexico. Like many Spanish **conquistadores**, Coronado wanted to find gold. After listening to de Niza's stories, he set out with around 300 Spanish troops and 1,000 enslaved Native Americans on an expedition to locate Cíbola.

During this journey, Coronado sent Garcia López de Cárdenas and 25 men to the west to find a great river that the Hopi people had described. They became the first Europeans to see the Grand Canyon. The Spaniards tried to descend the cliffs of the canyon to reach the river below, but they could not reach the bottom. The cliffs were too steep.

Coronado and his men continued east until they finally reached Kansas. They never found any gold, but they encountered a number of Native people. Coronado's men stole food and clothing from the Pueblo people. Cárdenas and his group set fire to 13 villages to discourage the Native people from rebelling.

Coronado's expedition came to an end with the Spanish believing there was no gold or silver in the area. Had they looked beneath the ground instead, they would have discovered great wealth. But they did not, and Spain lost interest in Arizona for nearly 40 years.

SPANISH RULE

In 1582, Spaniard Antonio de Espejo visited the Hopi Nation. Espejo convinced the Hopi people that the Spaniards posed no threat. He received gifts of hundreds of woven cotton blankets. Espejo listened to tales about a lake of gold found farther west. The stories proved false, but he did find silver deposits.

MINI-BIO

FRANCISCO VÁSQUEZ DE CORONADO: CONQUISTADOR

Francisco Vásquez de Coronado (1510–1554) was born in Spain and moved to Mexico in 1535, where he served as a governor. From 1540 to 1542, he led an expedition across the Southwest and onto the Great Plains in search of the legendary Seven Cities of Gold. Coronado's search ended at a Wichita village somewhere in today's Kansas. Discouraged, he returned to Mexico, where he was considered a failure. He again became a governor, but he was soon charged with brutality toward the Native people and was removed from office. He spent his last years in Mexico City.

Want to know more? Visit www.factsfornow.scholastic.com and enter the keyword **Arizona**.

Spanish explorers visited Hopi villages like this one in search of gold, silver, and other riches.

Espejo later reported to Spanish officials about his discovery of valuable metals in New Mexico, which then included Arizona. His discovery renewed Spain's interest in New Mexico, but no immediate action was taken. Many years later, in 1598, Spain named Juan de Oñate governor of New Mexico. Oñate led hundreds of people and thousands of cattle up the Rio Grande. About 20 miles (32 km) from today's Santa Fe, they established the first lasting European settlement in New Mexico.

A troop of Oñate's men led by Captain Marco Farfán de los Godos visited a Hopi village, where they heard about a silver mine that Native people were working. They decided to investigate. Within two years, Farfán managed to locate much of the region's mineral wealth.

THE PUEBLO REVOLT

In addition to conquistadores, Spain also sent Roman Catholic priests to Arizona to bring European religion and customs to the Native people. The **missionaries** first arrived in Hopi villages in 1629. Ignoring the fact that the Hopis already had their own religion, the priests insisted that the Hopi people convert to Catholicism, attend church, and dress in European-style clothing.

The missionaries and conquistadores also brought diseases with them. Native Americans had never before encountered smallpox, measles, chicken pox, and other diseases common to Europeans. Because their bodies were not accustomed to these diseases, they could not fight them off. European diseases swept through the Native American population, sometimes wiping out entire villages.

WORD TO KNOW

missionaries *people who try to convert others to a religion*

The Tumacácori Mission in southern Arizona was established in 1691.

MINI-BIO

EUSEBIO KINO: PRIEST ON HORSEBACK

As a priest, Eusebio Francisco Kino (1644–1711) dreamed of carrying the Catholic religion to China, but the church sent him to Mexico instead. In addition to being a priest, Kino was a mathematician, an astronomer, and a mapmaker. He was the first person to draw accurate maps of Pimería Alta. In 1687, Kino began working with the Pima people and establishing missions in Arizona. He worked to improve the way the Spanish treated the Pima people. He remained a missionary until his death in 1711. A statue of him (above) stands in Hermosillo in Sonora, Mexico.

? **Want to know more?** Visit www.factsfornow .scholastic.com and enter the keyword **Arizona**.

WORD TO KNOW

missions *places created by a religious group to spread its beliefs*

The Spanish built churches and homes and demanded that the Native people work for them. In 1680, Hopis and the Pueblo people of New Mexico rebelled, trying to rid their land of the Spanish. The leaders of the revolt planned well. The Native forces swooped down on European settlements along the Rio Grande, driving out all of the foreigners. The Spanish conquered New Mexico again in 1692, but they never retook Hopi lands.

KINO AND HIS MISSIONS

In Pimería Alta, in what is now southern Arizona, Spanish settlers treated Native Americans brutally, forcing them to work long hours in mines. But in 1687, a different kind of European arrived. An Italian priest named Eusebio Kino traveled on horseback from one village to the next. He founded 25 **missions** in Arizona and Mexico, including Tumacácori and San Xavier del Bac. Kino disapproved of the way the Spanish treated the Native people. He instead treated them with respect and kindness.

Most Europeans in the region treated the Native Americans badly. They demanded free labor, took land and silver, and ignored the Native people's customs and traditions. However, they also introduced new foods and tools that improved the Native Americans' lives in some ways.

During the 1740s, the Pima people grew increasingly angry over the Spaniards' behavior. In 1751, Pima

In 1700, the Mission San Xavier del Bac was founded by Father Eusebio Kino. The mission was later moved a few miles south, and the new structure (shown above) was completed in 1797.

leader Captain-General Luís Oacpicagigua led his people in a rebellion. Within a few days, they had killed more than 100 Spanish settlers, miners, and ranchers. The Pima Revolt lasted four months before Oacpicagigua surrendered. After that, the Spaniards began establishing forts, called presidios, to protect themselves from further attacks.

As the 19th century approached, the Spanish continued to mistreat the Native Americans in Arizona, and the Native Americans continued to fight back. But there were distant rumblings of change. On the East Coast of North America, a new country was being born. In the coming decades, the United States would spread across the continent.

READ ABOUT

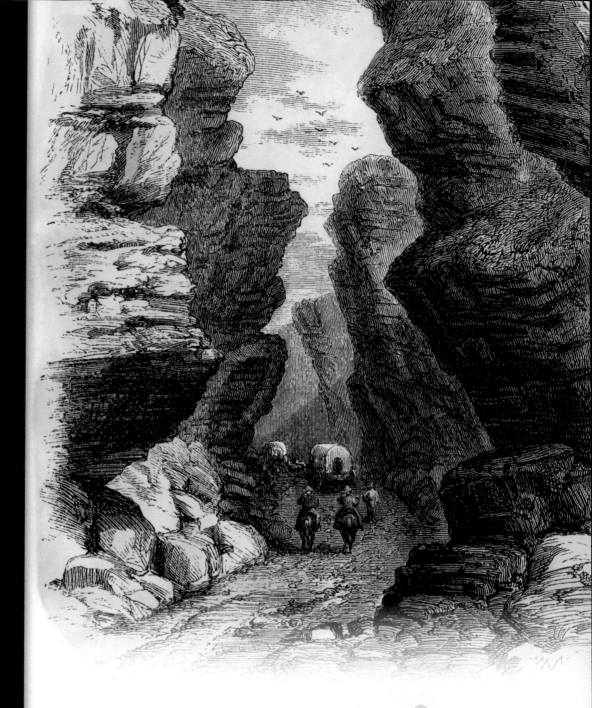

Covered wagons
passing through
the Canyon of San
Felipe, mid-1800s

1821

*Mexico wins
independence
from Spain*

1848

*The United States takes
control of northern
Arizona at the end of the
Mexican-American War*

◄**1853**

*Gold is reportedly
found in the
Colorado River*

GROWTH AND CHANGE

★

THE UNITED STATES PURCHASED THE LOUISIANA TERRITORY IN 1803. Gaining this area, in the center of the continent, allowed the nation to begin spreading west toward the Pacific Ocean. The fact that Native Americans had long lived on the land and that some European nations now claimed it was ignored.

1863

Arizona Territory is established

1860s–70s ▶
Cochise leads Chiricahua Apaches in a fight against white settlement

1881

The Earps fight the Clanton gang in the gunfight at the OK Corral

The U.S. Army fighting along the Mexican border in 1846

THE MEXICAN-AMERICAN WAR

The United States was established when it successfully fought for its independence from Great Britain. Similarly, Mexico wanted to be free from Spain. The fight for Mexican independence began in 1810. Mexico finally won its independence in 1821, after 11 years of war.

The new government in Mexico faced serious problems. The nation was deep in debt, and Mexican mines, ranches, and farms had not been productive for years. Mexico wanted to ease the country's economic problems and to increase the population of Texas. So Mexico's government invited U.S. citizens to settle in Texas, which was then part of Mexico. Texas began filling with slaveholders, who brought with them a cotton-based economy.

Many of these new Texans did not want their territory to be part of Mexico. In 1836, Texas became an independent nation, and less than a decade later, it joined the United States. By 1846, the United States, driven by the desire to expand its territories to the Pacific Ocean, declared war on Mexico because the Mexican government would not sell land that the U.S. government wanted. During the war, two U.S. Army battalions marched into northern Arizona, taking control of it. The war ended in 1848, when Mexico and the United States signed the Treaty of Guadalupe Hidalgo.

Under the treaty, the United States gained half of Mexico's land in return for $15 million. The land added to the United States included today's California, Nevada, Utah, most of Arizona and New Mexico, and parts of Colorado and Wyoming. Mexico agreed to sell the United States a strip of land called the Gadsden Purchase in 1853, giving Arizona and New Mexico their present borders.

BOOM TOWNS

The United States took control of the Southwest just before the California gold rush began in 1849. Suddenly, thousands of hopeful miners and their families headed west on wagon trains. A few years later, Arizona had a gold rush of its own. In 1853, Francis Aubry reported that he had found gold in the Colorado River. Five years later, a major gold rush began when Jacob Snively and a group of miners struck gold on the Gila River, not far from its junction with the Colorado. Miners rushed to Arizona, hoping to strike it rich.

In weeks, a town sprang up where there had been nothing. Journalist J. Ross Browne described the scene: "Enterprising men hurried to the spot with barrels of whiskey and billiard tables; . . . traders crowded in with wagon-loads of pork and beans. . . . There was everything in Gila City within a few months but a church and a jail."

Panning for gold

48

Picture Yourself . . .

as a Woman in an Arizona Mining Town

When your husband decided to move the family to Arizona so that he could search for gold, you had little say in the matter. Now, you are living in a mining town. You share a tent with your husband and two children. There is little water, so after you wash dishes, you use the same water to bathe yourself and the children and then wash the clothes. The remaining water, filthy and soapy, is used to water the garden you scrape out of the soil. You have many jobs to do as a wife and mother in the Arizona wilderness. You are a cook, baker, laundress, teacher, nurse . . . the list goes on and on. You have been in Arizona nearly three months, and you are exhausted. As summer approaches, you are worried. How will your family survive in the blazing heat without water?

People moved to Arizona by wagon train, and the trip was difficult. Most people walked to make it easier on the horses or mules pulling the wagons. Water was hard to come by, and many animals did not survive the trip. In 1849, Louisiana Strentzel wrote in her diary, "We found that the only way to get through was to travel slowly in the cool of the day, save the animals as much as possible and stop at every little grass we could find. . . . In one stretch of 16 miles [26 km], I counted 27 dead animals immediately by the road, besides those that wandered off in search of water and died."

Esteban Ochoa came to the Arizona territory in the 1850s. A native of Sonora, Mexico, he was a businessman

The arrival of white settlers and the building of railroads forced many Native Americans off their land.

who also ran a freight service to deliver goods throughout the region. He went on to be mayor of Tucson and later served in the territorial government. Another business leader from Sonora was Mariano Samaniego. He became a U.S. citizen after the Gadsden Purchase and graduated from Saint Louis University. Moving to Tucson in the 1860s, he was a freighter, cattle rancher, and merchant. He went on to be a respected public official for the territory.

People flooded into Arizona from around the nation and around the world in hopes of striking it rich. Many African American men moved to the mining towns to start new lives. Other African American pioneers in Arizona became stagecoach drivers, cowboys, and lawmen.

PUSHED ASIDE

As more and more white miners, shop owners, and other settlers moved into Arizona, Native Americans were pushed aside. They were forced to sign treaties with the government and move onto reservations. In 1859, Congress established Gila River Indian Community, the first of many Native American reservations. The reservation, which still exists today, lies 40 miles (64 km) south of Phoenix and is home to members of the Akimel O'odham and Pee-Posh nations.

Reservation life was difficult. Native Americans could not hunt off the reservation, but all too often the reservation land could not support them. The government said it would provide food, blankets, and shelter, but this did not always happen. Many Native Americans struggled to survive.

BECOMING A TERRITORY

Arizona was growing rapidly as mining towns sprang up overnight. Soon, people in Arizona were urging the U.S. Congress to declare Arizona a separate territory—it had

FAQ

Q8 HOW BIG IS THE GILA RIVER INDIAN COMMUNITY?

A8 The reservation is 372,000 acres (151,000 ha) and today is home to some 14,000 people.

been part of New Mexico Territory since 1850. President Abraham Lincoln created Arizona Territory in 1863.

By this time, the conflict between the North and the South over slavery and states' rights had exploded into the Civil War (1861–1865). Though much of the war was fought in the eastern part of the country, Arizona saw conflicts such as the Battle of Picacho Peak.

NATIVE AMERICAN RESISTANCE

White settlers continued to pour into Arizona, but some Native Americans were fighting back against the invasion of their lands. Apaches attacked mining towns and white settlements. They ambushed wagon trains as they crossed Arizona. With most of the U.S. military involved in the Civil War, few soldiers remained in Arizona to protect white towns from Native American raids.

White settlers most feared the Chiricahua leader Mangas Coloradas (Red Sleeves) and his son-in-law Cochise. Mangas Coloradas was an accomplished leader of the Native American resistance. He was tall and muscular, with long, thick hair that hung down to his waist.

In 1863, Mangas Coloradas went to a U.S. fort to discuss peace. Instead, he was captured, tortured, and shot. His captors mutilated his body. They cut off his head and shipped it to the Smithsonian Institution in Washington, D.C., to be studied. Apaches were outraged. Much later, an Apache named James Kaywaykla said, "The killing of an unarmed man who has gone to an enemy under truce was an incomprehensible act, but infinitely worse was the mutilation of his body. . . . Little did the White [people] know how they would pay when they **defiled** the body of our great chief!"

Cochise and other Apache leaders fought the people who intruded on their land, trying to force them to leave.

CAPITAL ON THE MOVE

When Arizona Territory was established in 1863, Prescott was chosen as the temporary capital. The capital moved to Tucson in 1867, back to Prescott in 1877, and finally to Phoenix in 1889, where it remains.

WORD TO KNOW

defiled *dishonored*

White settlers by the thousands continued to stream across Apache land. They used up water sources. They ate food and slaughtered game the Apaches relied on. The Apaches began to attack groups of settlers. They stole cattle so that they could eat.

The Apaches were tired of war, tired of losing their land. They were hungry. An Apache leader named Eskiminzin sent a handful of women to Camp Grant, a military outpost north of Tucson, to speak to the officer in charge about peace. In exchange for food and protection, a group of Apaches was hired to help on local farms. The Apaches set up a camp just east of Camp Grant.

Some people blamed every problem in the area on Apaches. A group of white settlers, Mexican Americans, and Tohono O'odhams organized a group of raiders. On April 30, 1871, they entered the Apache encampment and murdered 118 Apaches, mostly women and children. In addition to those murdered, 28 Apache infants were taken and sold as slaves. This event is today known as the Camp Grant Massacre.

The raiders were caught and put on trial. After five days of hearing witnesses to the massacre, the all-male

MINI-BIO

GERONIMO: DEFENDER OF HIS PEOPLE

Though not a chief of the Apache, Geronimo (1829–1909) has a special place in Native American history. In 1858, Mexican forces attacked his camp and killed his wife, mother, and children. As a military and spiritual leader, Geronimo waged war on Mexican and U.S. forces in hopes of defending his land and people. His narrow escapes are legendary. Once he hid in a cave that U.S. troops guarded, then mysteriously appeared in a nearby area. And it is said that he evaded some 5,000 U.S. troops for more than a year. He finally surrendered in 1886, marking the end of Native American resistance in the United States. In his later years, Geronimo became a celebrity, appearing at the 1904 World's Fair and riding in President Theodore Roosevelt's inaugural parade in 1905. But he died of pneumonia while living at Fort Sill, Oklahoma, as a prisoner of war. He never returned to his homeland.

? **Want to know more?** Visit www.factsfornow .scholastic.com and enter the keyword **Arizona**.

52

MINI-BIO

COCHISE: APACHE LEADER

Cochise (1812–1874) was a chief of the Chiricahua Apaches, a fearless fighter who successfully led his people in battles against the white settlers. After years of fighting the newcomers, he became friends with Thomas Jeffords, a government official. Jeffords arranged peace talks between the Apache people and the U.S. Army. The government had planned to send the Chiricahua Apache people to a reservation hundreds of miles from their homeland. But Cochise objected. He wanted his people to live on their traditional lands. The government agreed, and Cochise and his people surrendered. But after Cochise died, the government moved his people to a different reservation.

❓ Want to know more? Visit www.factsfornow .scholastic.com and enter the keyword **Arizona**.

jury took only 19 minutes to reach a verdict. All involved in the slaughter were found "not guilty."

Meanwhile, Cochise and other Apaches continued to fight the U.S. Army. The army began using other Native Americans as scouts to hunt Apaches in their mountain homes. Finally, Cochise surrendered so that his people would survive.

BUFFALO SOLDIERS AND OUTLAWS

After the Civil War ended, the U.S. government turned its attention to rebuilding the South and ending Native American resis-

Among other duties, Buffalo Soldiers were used to escort mail carriers and protect stagecoaches.

Think About It

Why would the head of a Native American nation lead his people into a prolonged war against great odds and greater arms? Think about what Cochise said as he was about to surrender to the U.S. Army:

When I was young I walked all over this country, east and west, and saw no other people than the Apaches. After many summers I walked again and found another race of people had come to take it. How is it?

We were once a large people covering these mountains. We lived well: we were at peace. . . . My people have killed Americans and Mexicans and taken their property. Their losses have been greater than mine. I have killed ten white men for every Indian slain, but I know that the whites are many and the Indians are few. Apaches are growing less every day.

Why is it that the Apaches wait to die—that they carry their lives on their fingernails? They roam over the hills and plains and want the heavens to fall on them. The Apaches were once a great nation; they are now but few, and because of this they want to die and so carry their lives on their fingernails.

I am alone in the world. I want to live in these mountains; I do not want to go to Tularosa. That is a long way off. I have drunk of the waters of the Dragoon Mountains and they have cooled me: I do not want to leave here.

Nobody wants peace more than I do. Why shut me up on a reservation? We will make peace; we will keep it faithfully. But let us go around free as Americans do. Let us go wherever we please.

tance to white settlement of the West. The government sent troops to occupy forts throughout Arizona. African American **cavalry** soldiers known as Buffalo Soldiers guarded some of these forts. The Buffalo Soldiers made up one-fifth of the entire U.S. Cavalry troops in the western territories. These U.S. troops ensured the safety of travelers. They protected stagecoaches and work crews building roads, laying railroad tracks, and stringing telegraph lines across Arizona.

WORD TO KNOW

cavalry *soldiers who ride on horseback*

The town of Tombstone in 1881

FAQ

Q8 HOW DID TOMBSTONE GET ITS NAME?

A8 In 1861, miner Ed Schlieffelin headed into Apache land in search of silver. U.S. soldiers warned Schlieffelin that all he would find would be a tombstone. Instead, he struck it rich, and other miners poured into the area. With a touch of humor, Schlieffelin named his blossoming town Tombstone. By 1881, Tombstone had 4,000 residents. It was the largest town between New Orleans, Louisiana, and San Francisco, California.

Some of Arizona's towns blossomed into cities. The increase in population and wealth attracted more businesses and better means of transportation. The Southern Pacific Railroad reached Tucson in 1880. By 1883, the Atlantic and Pacific Railroad traveled from Albuquerque, New Mexico, to Flagstaff, Arizona.

Wealth attracted criminals, too. Gangs of outlaws robbed trains, stagecoaches, and banks. Some gangs were so violent that people sometimes feared walking down the sidewalks in their towns. The Clanton gang, also known as the Cowboys, operated along the Mexican border. They were cattle rustlers, stagecoach robbers, and murderers. The Clantons were based in Tombstone, a booming mining town in southeastern Arizona. They made living in Tombstone miserable.

Tombstone was one of the wildest towns in the Wild West. Gamblers and outlaws filled its streets. In 1881, Tombstone's town marshal, Virgil Earp, his brother Wyatt, and others fought the Clanton gang. Although the event is now known as the Gunfight at the OK Corral, it actually took place in a vacant lot in town. After a brief hail of bullets, the fight was over. Three members of the Clanton gang had been shot dead.

As the 1800s came to an end, so did the days of the Wild West. Arizona was changing greatly at the dawn of the 20th century. Silver and gold mining declined in importance, but copper mining boomed. Soon, Arizona would become a state.

MINI-BIO

WYATT EARP: OLD WEST LAWMAN

Wyatt Earp (1848–1929) was one of the Earp brothers, a family of gunfighters and lawmen. Earp was born in Illinois. At 15, he tried to enlist in the army, but he was too young. He was a gunslinger and a buffalo hunter before becoming a legendary lawman in Kansas. In 1879, he moved to Tombstone with his brothers. After he fought the Clanton gang, which was terrorizing Tombstone's citizens, many people considered him a hero. Dozens of movies and television programs have been made about Earp.

? **Want to know more?** Visit www.factsfornow .scholastic.com and enter the keyword **Arizona**.

56

READ ABOUT

A busy street in
Bisbee, early 1900s

1906

*Construction
begins on
the Theodore
Roosevelt Dam*

▲ **1912**

*Arizona
becomes the
48th state*

1917

*Mine owners
ship 1,200
striking workers
into the desert*

1942–1945

*Japanese Americans
are confined in
internment camps in
Arizona*

CHAPTER FIVE

MORE MODERN TIMES

★

IN THE LATE 1800S, COPPER BECAME BIG BUSINESS IN ARIZONA. Copper-mining towns such as Bisbee, Jerome, and Morenci were booming. Services for refining, selling, and shipping the ore bolstered the state's economy. As the state became more industrial, it began to shed its Wild West image. And as the 20th century dawned, Arizona remained a territory and was home to 123,000 people. Those people wanted statehood.

1950s
Lawsuits challenging discrimination are filed by people of color

1994 ▲
César Chávez receives the Presidential Medal of Freedom

2010
Arizona passes a strict anti-immigration law

President William Howard Taft (seated) signing Arizona into statehood, 1912

WORD TO KNOW

recalled *removed from office*

STATEHOOD AND GROWTH

In 1910, the U.S. Congress passed a bill that would allow Arizona to hold a constitutional convention. The following year, the people of Arizona approved a constitution, but Arizona still was not a state.

Although the U.S. Congress approved of statehood for Arizona, President William Howard Taft refused to accept Arizona's new constitution. Taft, who had once been a judge, did not like that this constitution allowed judges to be **recalled**. He would not allow Arizona to become a state until it changed its constitution.

The change was made, and on February 14, 1912, President Taft signed the proclamation making Arizona the 48th state. Shortly after achieving statehood, Arizona's voters changed their constitution to once again make judges subject to recall. Taft may not have liked the situation, but it was too late.

Arizona: From Territory to Statehood

(1863–1912)

This map shows the original Arizona territory and the area that became the state of Arizona in 1912.

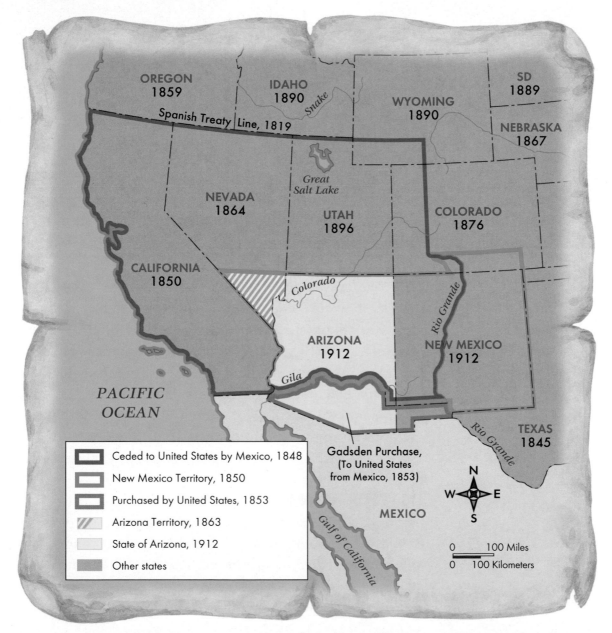

OREGON 1859

IDAHO 1890

SD 1889

WYOMING 1890

NEBRASKA 1867

Spanish Treaty Line, 1819

Snake

Great Salt Lake

NEVADA 1864

UTAH 1896

COLORADO 1876

CALIFORNIA 1850

Colorado

ARIZONA 1912

NEW MEXICO 1912

Rio Grande

PACIFIC OCEAN

Gila

TEXAS 1845

Rio Grande

Gadsden Purchase,
(To United States
from Mexico, 1853)

MEXICO

Gulf of California

Ceded to United States by Mexico, 1848

New Mexico Territory, 1850

Purchased by United States, 1853

Arizona Territory, 1863

State of Arizona, 1912

Other states

N W E S

0   100 Miles
0   100 Kilometers

The Theodore Roosevelt Dam was completed in 1911.

Originally, the Theodore Roosevelt Dam was 356 feet (109 m) tall. In 1911, it was the tallest **masonry** dam ever built.

WORDS TO KNOW

reservoirs *artificial lakes or tanks created for water storage*

masonry *made of stone or brick*

Arizona was growing quickly, but it was plagued by a lack of water. The federal government began building dams that would create **reservoirs** to hold water for drinking and irrigation. The first major dams were built along the Salt River. Work on the Theodore Roosevelt Dam began in 1906 and took five years. Dams on the Colorado River soon followed. The increase in irrigation water made farming much more successful. Between 1910 and 1920, farm acreage in Arizona increased by 400 percent.

IN THE MINES

As copper mining boomed in Arizona, mine owners got rich. Mine workers, meanwhile, had hot, dirty, dangerous jobs and struggled to survive on low wages. Beginning in 1905, some joined a labor union dedicated to improving working conditions for miners. Conflicts continuously

arose between union organizers and mine owners who disliked unions.

In 1917, the union arranged a **strike** in Bisbee and Jerome. Mine owners in Bisbee, with the help of the local sheriff and many armed men, rounded up more than 1,200 striking miners. They loaded the miners onto railroad cars and shipped them into the New Mexico desert several hundred miles away. They were dumped there without money. New Mexico officials gave the men food and tents to sleep in, but the sheriff of Bisbee refused to let them return to their homes. After this, the strike effort crumbled.

ANGELA HAMMER: NEWSPAPER PIONEER

Angela Hutchinson Hammer (1870–1952) was born in a Nevada mining town and moved to Arizona when she was nine years old. As a young woman, she got a taste of being involved with a newspaper—she set type by hand. After marrying, she bought the *Wickenburg Miner* newspaper in 1904. From 1907 to 1913, Hammer moved from one mining town to another, establishing small newspapers in each one. She struggled to make a success of her papers, often facing money problems. Despite the difficulties, she later said that her "happiest days were spent in the middle of a hot controversy as editor of a local newspaper." Hammer was elected to the Arizona Newspapers Association Hall of Fame in 1965.

? **Want to know more?** Visit www.factsfornow .scholastic.com and enter the keyword **Arizona**.

WORD TO KNOW

strike *an organized refusal to work, usually as a sign of protest about working conditions*

These miners, who went on strike in 1917, were sent into the desert.

Civil Works Administration workers building a hospital in Tempe

PROSPERITY AND DEPRESSION

That same year, the United States entered World War I (1914–1918), which was already raging in Europe. The war effort increased demand for copper, beef, and crops, boosting Arizona's economy. As the state's economy flourished, cities grew. The young state was prospering.

The good times did not last, however. In 1929, the United States plunged into the Great Depression, the worst economic downturn in the nation's history. Banks, factories, and stores closed. Farmers could not sell their crops, and many could not afford to keep their land. All across the United States, people lost their jobs.

In 1933, Franklin D. Roosevelt became president of the United States. Roosevelt started a group of programs called the New Deal to pull the United States out of the Depression and put citizens back to work. New Deal programs hired workers to build schools, dams, roads, and libraries. Unemployed writers were paid to produce state histories, and unemployed artists were paid to paint murals on post office walls. Young Arizonans went to work building trails and visitor centers in parks around the state. But while the New Deal helped Americans survive the Great Depression, it did not bring the economy out of its slump.

WORLD WAR II

In 1939, Germany invaded Poland, and Great Britain and France declared war on Germany. World War II had begun. The United States joined the war in 1941, after Japan, an ally of Germany, bombed the U.S. naval base at Pearl Harbor, Hawai'i.

The war effort finally put Arizonans and all Americans back to work. Suddenly, farm products were in high

These two Navajo code talkers worked with a marine regiment in the Pacific during World War II.

THE NAVAJO CODE TALKERS

During World War II, the U.S. military communicated important orders by radio. The military sent the messages in code, but the Japanese often broke the codes—that is, until some Navajo marines began making the codes. Only a handful of non-Navajos in the world spoke the Navajo language, so no one could understand the words, much less break the code. The Navajo "code talkers" created one of the few codes that the Japanese never broke. The code talkers helped the United States win many battles in the Pacific, but the military kept their existence a secret. So when the war ended, Navajos returning home received no medals, honors, or parades. In 2000, the original code talkers received Congressional Gold Medals from the president as belated recognition for their aid in winning World War II.

demand. Beef cattle earned record prices. Arizona's copper was also in great demand. Factories opened their doors and hired workers to fill two and three shifts daily. As men joined the military, women took their places on the assembly lines. The military built air bases and training camps in Arizona.

After the United States and Japan went to war, some Americans feared that Japanese Americans might be spying for the Japanese government. In 1942, all along the West Coast, loyal American citizens of Japanese descent were rounded up. They were forced to leave their jobs and schools, and they were confined in **internment camps**. Two of these camps were in Arizona. Meanwhile, other Japanese Americans volunteered to serve in the army. Many fought and died for their country.

WORD TO KNOW

internment camps *places where people are confined, usually during wartime*

The corner of Main and 12th streets in the city of Douglas, 1950s

AFTER THE WAR

In 1940, the state had just under a half million people. By 1960, that number had nearly tripled. Part of the reason for this explosion in population was the arrival of air-conditioning. After World War II, air-conditioning became common in homes, making the state and its blistering summers more appealing to people. Many more tourists also traveled to Arizona to explore its deserts and canyons and enjoy the mild winter weather.

Arizona's rapid population growth created serious water problems. For many years, much of Arizona's water resources were diverted to California. In 1973, however, Arizona began construction on the Central Arizona Project (CAP), a $3.6 billion network of canals, tunnels, dams, and pumping stations to bring water from the Colorado River to Arizona's cities and towns.

CAP will not end Arizona's water problems. The state's population stands at more than 6 million people, and it is expected to top 8 million by 2025. Where will Arizona get the water to meet its population's needs? It is hoped that conservation measures such as recycling used water and processing river water will help ease the water burden on the state.

CIVIL RIGHTS

As Arizona grew, Arizonans of a variety of backgrounds began a determined battle to win equal rights for everyone. African Americans had lived in Arizona since pioneer times. By the time Arizona became a state, many African Americans had settled in cities such as Phoenix, Tucson, and Flagstaff. Newspapers that covered the African American community followed. By World War II, many African Americans in Arizona had joined professions such as medicine and law. In 1950, two African Americans were elected to the Arizona legislature.

At this time, schools in Arizona were **segregated**. In the 1950s, people of color began filing lawsuits challenging such **discrimination**. The case of *Baca v. Winslow* resulted from the city of Winslow's policy of banning Mexican Americans, Native Americans, and African Americans from using the public swimming pool on some days. The city bowed to pressure and changed its policy. In the case of *Ortiz v. Jack,* the Glendale Board of Education agreed to stop discriminating against and segregating Mexican American children. In the case of *Gonzalez v. Sheely,* a judge ruled that segregating Mexican Americans in public schools was illegal. The lawsuits opened new doors for people of color in Arizona. Universities developed programs for Latino and Chicano studies. Mexican Americans became involved in politics, and many sought political office.

CIVIL RIGHTS LEADER

George Brooks spent decades fighting for civil rights for all Arizonans. His civil rights campaigns united African Americans with Latino and white community leaders. Brooks confronted leading Arizona employers, demanding that people of color have equal access to jobs. In 1964, he traveled to Washington, D.C., where he tried to convince lawmakers to fund a preschool program. His idea became part of the successful Head Start program. He also launched a "Meals on Wheels" program to feed the elderly in Phoenix. Brooks served in the state legislature, and Phoenix named an elementary school in his honor. New leaders today continue to be inspired by his courage and hard work.

WORDS TO KNOW

segregated *separated from others according to race, class, ethnic group, religion, or other factors*

discrimination *unequal treatment based on race, gender, religion, or other factors*

CÉSAR CHÁVEZ: LABOR LEADER

César Chávez (1927–1993) was born near Yuma and raised on a small farm. As a young man, he became upset by the plight of migrant farmworkers. The farmworkers moved frequently, picking crops for little pay. In 1962, Chávez founded the National Farm Workers Association, which later became the United Farm Workers. He encouraged union members to go on strike to improve pay rates and conditions for migrant workers. He succeeded in getting better wages, health care, and better living conditions for farmworkers. In 1994, Chávez was awarded the Presidential Medal of Freedom, one of the nation's highest honors.

❓ Want to know more? Visit www.factsfornow.scholastic.com and enter the keyword **Arizona**.

WORD TO KNOW

undocumented *lacking documents required for legal immigration or residence*

Despite these changes, discrimination continued. Farmers paid Mexican American migrant workers little money and provided them with inadequate housing. In 1984, Phelps Dodge, an Arizona mining company, ordered its Mexican American employees to stop speaking Spanish in the lunchrooms and workplaces. The employees stated that they were being treated unfairly, and eventually, Phelps Dodge reversed its order.

ARIZONA TODAY

By the end of the 20th century, Arizona was among the fastest-growing states in the nation. Many people moved to the state, part of a region called the Sun Belt, because of its sunny year-round weather. Other people, including **undocumented**, or illegal, immigrants who cross the border from Mexico, came for a chance at a better life. In 2010, about 460,000 undocumented immigrants lived in Arizona. Some Arizonans believe this puts a strain on government services such as hospitals. Others fear that illegal immigrants commit crimes. The state responded to residents' concerns with strict immigration legislation.

In 2007, the state legislature passed laws that fined employers if they hired illegal immigrants. Other laws prevented undocumented immigrants from using public services. In 2010, the Arizona legislature passed State Bill 1070 (SB 1070), one of the toughest anti-immigrant laws in the nation. The law stated that all noncitizens more than 14 years old who remain in the United States longer than 30 days have to register with the U.S. government. The law also required noncitizens to always carry registration documents with them. It was a crime for them to be without the documents. Law enforcement officials were also given the power to stop and question anyone they believed to be an illegal immigrant.

Many Americans believe Arizona's tough new immigration laws unfairly target minority groups, especially Latinos, and could lead to an alarming rise in civil rights violations. Many thousands of people demonstrated against the law at rallies in cities throughout the country. In a series of court actions, the U.S. federal government filed lawsuits to have the Arizona law struck down. In 2012, the U.S. Supreme Court ruled that some parts of SB 1070 were too harsh. The ruling allowed police to investigate the immigration status of someone they stopped, but it disallowed the part of the law that made it a crime for an immigrant not to carry registration documents.

Immigration will continue to be an important issue in Arizona, as will the state's urgent need for water. But most Arizonans are optimistic about their state's future. Arizona has long been a place where different cultures mingled, and people moved to start their lives anew. It continues to be a sunny beacon for many people looking for new opportunities and better lives.

MINI-BIO

LORI PIESTEWA: HOPI SOLDIER

Lori Ann Piestewa (1981–2003) was a member of the Hopi tribe from Tuba City. Piestewa, whose Hopi name was Kocha-Hon-Mana (White Bear Girl), was 22 years old when she was sent to Iraq as a member of the U.S. Army. Her unit took a wrong turn and was attacked. She became the first American woman killed in the Iraq War. She is also believed to be the first Native American woman killed in combat on foreign soil.

? **Want to know more?** Visit www.facts fornow.scholastic.com and enter the keyword **Arizona**.

READ ABOUT

Diamondbacks
fans cheer on their
team at Chase
Field in Phoenix.

CHAPTER SIX

PEOPLE

★

A YOUNG WOMAN ON HORSEBACK RIDES AMID TOWERING RED ROCK FORMATIONS IN NORTHEASTERN ARIZONA. No matter which way she looks, she does not see another soul. Farther south, in Phoenix, some 50,000 fans pack a baseball stadium for an Arizona Diamondbacks game. It will be a great game, but fans are likely to sit in a traffic jam on the way home. Arizona is a blend of wide-open spaces and crowded cities in the middle of the desert.

Phoenix is home to people from all over the world.

Big City Life

This list shows the population of Arizona's biggest cities.

Phoenix 1,445,632
Tucson 520,116
Mesa 439,041
Chandler 226,721
Glendale 236,123

Source: U.S. Census Bureau, 2010 census

WHO LIVES IN ARIZONA?

Arizona has been among the fastest-growing states in recent years. Between 2010 and 2012, the state population increased by 2.5 percent. Some of these newcomers are retired people who moved to Arizona to enjoy the mild winters. Many of them spend only part of the year in Arizona, leaving when the weather turns hot.

The vast majority, some 90 percent, of Arizonans live in cities. City life in Arizona involves traffic jams, high-priced housing, and a shortage of water. In rural areas, there are no traffic problems and housing is cheaper, but there is still a shortage of water.

About 58 percent of the people in Arizona say they are white. Most trace their ancestry to Germany, England, or Ireland. About 30 percent of Arizonans are Latino, or Hispanic. Arizona was once part of Mexico, and most of the state's Latinos are of Mexican descent. Evidence of

Where Arizonans Live

The colors on this map indicate population density throughout the state.
The darker the color, the more people live there.

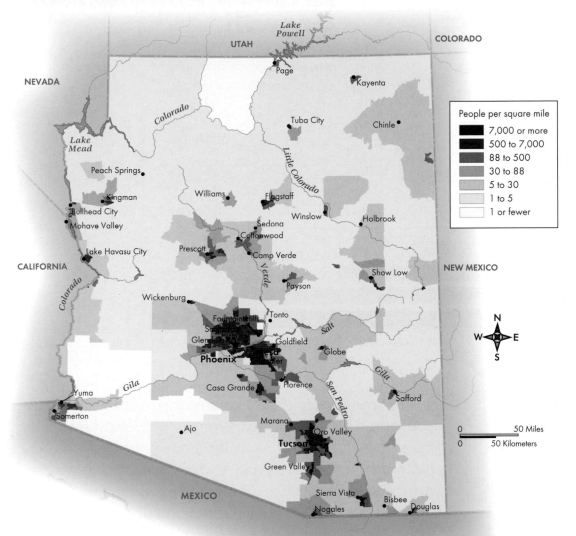

this history abounds in Arizona—from the spicy foods to
the mariachi bands playing at *quinceañera* parties to the
many Spanish-language radio stations. An estimated 20
percent of Arizonans speak Spanish at home.

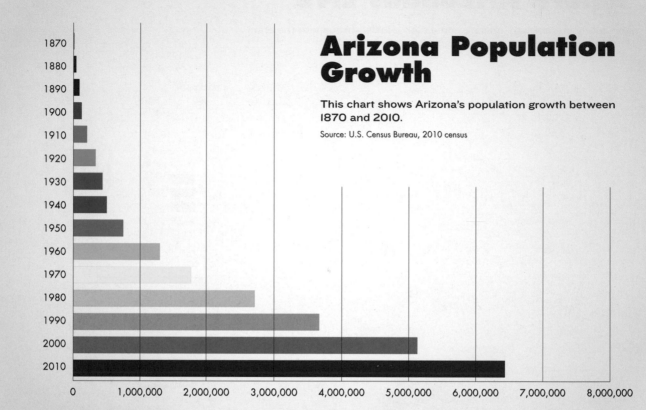

Arizona Population Growth

This chart shows Arizona's population growth between 1870 and 2010.

Source: U.S. Census Bureau, 2010 census

A sign for Mexican food in Tucson

African Americans make up 3.8 percent of Arizona's population. In recent years, many African Americans have moved to Arizona from midwestern and northeastern states. Phoenix and Tucson have sizable African American communities. Chinese people came to Arizona in the 1800s to work in mines and on railroads. In recent years, Asian immigrants are more likely to come from countries such as Vietnam, Cambodia, and Laos.

Arizona has the third-largest Native American and Alaska Native populations among the states, about 297,000 people. Arizona's Native Americans belong to many different nations, each with its own leadership, history, and traditions.

Dancers at a powwow in Phoenix

The Navajo Nation has around 174,000 members, making it the largest Native American nation. The Navajo Reservation covers 27,000 square miles (70,000 sq km). It lies mostly in northeastern Arizona but spreads into New Mexico and Utah. The reservation has its own police and fire departments. It has stores, libraries, and schools. Children in Navajo schools learn both the English and Navajo languages and are taught the responsibilities of citizenship in both nations.

Many Navajos wear traditional clothing for ceremonies and cultural or family events. A Navajo woman's traditional clothing includes moccasins, a pleated velvet or cotton skirt, and a long-sleeve blouse. She might also wear a sash belt, silver jewelry, and a handmade shawl. Traditional Navajo men's clothing includes velvet shirts and silver jewelry. Other times, Navajos dress like most other Arizonans—they wear jeans and boots.

FAQ

Q8 WHAT IS A QUINCEAÑERA?

A8 When a Mexican American girl turns 15, she celebrates her quinceañera. Family, friends, and relatives gather for this coming-of-age event.

People QuickFacts

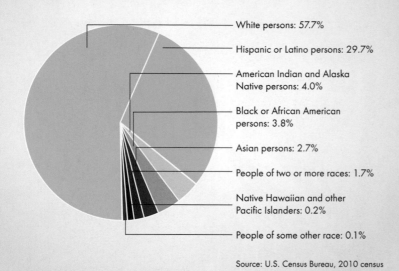

White persons: 57.7%

Hispanic or Latino persons: 29.7%

American Indian and Alaska Native persons: 4.0%

Black or African American persons: 3.8%

Asian persons: 2.7%

People of two or more races: 1.7%

Native Hawaiian and other Pacific Islanders: 0.2%

People of some other race: 0.1%

Source: U.S. Census Bureau, 2010 census

WORD TO KNOW

mesas *flat-topped hills*

Q: WHAT TIME IS IT IN ARIZONA?

A: Spring ahead? Fall back? Not in Arizona! When everyone else in the nation adjusts their clocks and watches to daylight saving time, Arizonans do not—except for the Navajo Reservation. The Navajo use daylight saving time. So, during the summer, when it's 11 A.M. in Window Rock, the capital of the Navajo Nation, it's 10 A.M. in Phoenix.

The Hopi people live in Hopi villages on the **mesas** in northeastern Arizona. Hopis are identified with their villages rather than with their nation as a whole. The village ties are so strong that Hopis in different villages speak different languages.

The Apache people live on a number of reservations. The two largest, the White Mountain Reservation and the San Carlos Reservation, are both in eastern Arizona. White Mountain Apaches often work in the logging and tourism businesses. Many San Carlos Apaches work as cowboys. This reservation produces more cowboys than any similar-sized region of Texas or Oklahoma. Each year, the San Carlos Rodeo attracts rodeo fans from throughout the Southwest.

The Tohono O'odham and Akimel O'odham (also called Pima) peoples live in the desert of southern Arizona. The O'odham peoples have traditionally been farmers, but in recent years, they have opened a resort on their land to attract tourists. Many people from the Hualapai and Havasupai tribes, which have reservations near the Grand Canyon, also work in tourism.

EDUCATION

Arizona has dozens of colleges, universities, and community colleges. The University of Arizona in Tucson is the state's oldest university. It has particularly strong astronomy and earth science departments. Other major universities in the state include Arizona State University and Northern Arizona University.

Arizona also has a network of community colleges that offer students an opportunity to attend a two-year program and then transfer to a four-year school. Many Native American reservations have community colleges. Diné College has two campuses on the Navajo Reservation. The school's mission is to promote higher education while maintaining the Navajo principles of harmony in all things. The college offers associate degrees in social sciences, art, early childhood education, public health, and environmental sciences, among others. Students can transfer credits to four-year college or university programs elsewhere.

Q: **WHAT IS ARIZONA'S MOST UNUSUAL COLLEGE?**

A: Most people would say the Arizona Cowboy College in Scottsdale. Classes include riding, roping, and shoeing. During the four-day course, students work side by side with cowboys on a real ranch.

Students at the University of Arizona

HOW TO TALK LIKE AN ARIZONAN

Traveling across Arizona, you'll hear a lot about "snow-birds." These aren't ice-loving penguins or perfectly white egrets. They're retired people who travel to Arizona in the winter to escape the cold weather in more northerly parts of the country. Many snowbirds like to explore Arizona's deserts. They might go for a hike in an arroyo (a dry riverbed), but they always keep an eye out for rattlers (rattlesnakes) among the rocks. After their hike, they might sit down and eat a sandwich on a sub roll (a long bun). By the time the monsoons (heavy summer rains) come, the snowbirds have long since headed back north.

HOW TO EAT LIKE AN ARIZONAN

A lot of food in Arizona reflects Mexican influences, which often means spicy. Arizonans take great pride in creating mouth-burning salsa (a tomato-based sauce) to serve with nachos, enchiladas, or other dishes. These salsas carry names such as Widowmaker, Attack of the Fire-Breathing Tomatoes, Heartburn Hotel, Your Hearse or Mine, the Great Burn, Fire in the Hole, and Ay-yay-yay-yay.

What makes these salsas so hot is the choice of chili peppers. Most salsas contain some amount of jalapeño—a relatively mild pepper. The really hot stuff includes habaneros—peppers hot enough to blister the tongue. Habaneros have so much firepower that pickers and chefs must wear gloves while handling the peppers to prevent burning their skin.

Chili peppers

MENU

WHAT'S ON THE MENU IN ARIZONA?

★ ★ ★

Tortilla chips

Cactus Fruit

Several types of cactus are edible. People eat the prickly pear fruit and pads. The fruit is sweet, sticky, and delicious with ice cream. The pads taste more like tart green beans or asparagus. Saguaro cactus fruit is eaten fresh and is often made into syrup and jelly.

Dil

Dil is a blood sausage made from sheep blood, potatoes, celery, sheep fat, onion, cornmeal, and spices. Navajos often serve it on holidays.

Menudo

This delicious dish, borrowed from Mexico, is a soup made from tripe (the stomach of a cow or other animal), green chilies, onions, and mint.

Jicama

Although jicama is a root vegetable, it belongs to the bean family. It is sweet, crisp, and tastes like an apple or a pear. Jicama is used in salads and stir-fry dishes.

Tomatillos

These relatives of tomatoes provide the color and tart flavor in many green Mexican sauces. They taste nothing like tomatoes. Tomatillos are used while they are still green—once they are ripe they are past their prime.

Tomatillos

TRY THIS RECIPE
Three-Cheese Nachos

Here's a quick and easy recipe that will please the whole family. Just be sure to have an adult nearby to help.

Ingredients:
1 large bag tortilla chips
2 cups Monterey Jack cheese, shredded
2 cups cheddar cheese, shredded
2 cups pepper jack cheese, shredded
½ cup green onions, chopped
1 cup onions, diced
1 cup canned corn, drained
1 small can green chilies, drained and diced
Salsa
Sour cream

Instructions:
1. Preheat the oven to 350°F.
2. Place half the tortilla chips in a 9 x 13-inch ovenproof pan.
3. Sprinkle half of the cheeses, onions, corn, and green chilies over the chips.
4. Add another layer of chips. Add the remaining cheeses, onions, corn, and chilies.
5. Bake for 15 to 20 minutes, or until the cheese is melted.
6. Serve with salsa and sour cream.

Joe Beeler, shown here in Sedona, was one of the founders of the Cowboy Artists of America.

Navajo rings

ART AND MUSIC

In 1964, three cowboys sat around a campfire and talked about their future. These men—Joe Beeler, Charlie Dye, and John Hampton—were Arizona artists, and they were going broke. They founded the Cowboy Artists of America, an organization that is now headquartered in Phoenix. Cowboy artists create paintings and sculptures of Native Americans and cowboys. Their annual art shows now attract collectors from across the globe.

Arizona's Native Americans have a long artistic tradition. Navajo and Hopi jewelry is often made from silver and turquoise. Traditional designs include squash blossoms, lizards, frogs, and tortoises. Necklaces, bracelets, and rings are popular, as are men's silver belt buckles and slides for bolo neckties, the state's official neckwear.

Basket making is another traditional craft. Some baskets are large and useful, while others are decorative and about the size of an egg. Baskets are made from a wide variety of materials, including horsehair, pine needles, and yucca fiber. Many Tohono O'odhams are superb basket weavers. They have an association dedicated to preserving the art of basketry.

Although it cannot be purchased, Navajo sand painting is remarkable for both its beauty and the patience it takes to create. The design is drawn on the ground and filled with colorful sand, bit by bit. Sand paintings are essential parts of many Navajo ceremonies and rituals.

Many Native Americans produce excellent pottery. Traditionally, the pottery is made by hand, not on a wheel. The decoration is painted on the clay using natural dyes, and the pot is fired over an open flame. The best handmade pottery can cost thousands of dollars.

Native American weavers produce rugs and blankets decorated with geometric designs or pictures. Navajo rugs, with their exquisite use of color and design, are highly prized by collectors.

Arizona has a rich musical history. Long ago, lonely cowboys sang ballads about their sweethearts, their

MINI-BIO

GENEVA RAMON: MASTER WEAVER

Geneva Ramon (?–) learned weaving by watching her father and grandmother when she was very young. Today, she weaves baskets using traditional Tohono O'odham themes such as mazes and dances. She makes some coiled baskets from the long leaves of yucca plants; others she makes from horsehair. She has won awards for her artistry at the Southwest Indian Art Fair and at the Celebration of Basketweaving. Ramon passes on her skills by teaching at a Tohono O'odham school.

? Want to know more? Visit www.facts fornow.scholastic.com and enter the keyword **Arizona**.

FAQ

Q8 WHAT IS A BOLO NECKTIE?

A8 It is a long leather strip held together at the neck by a metal, wooden, or stone slide.

Mariachi musicians prepare for a performance in Tucson.

favorite horses, or their herds of cattle. Cowboy ballads still have a place in Arizona. The state's official balladeer is Dolan Ellis. He writes original tunes, including some about Maricopa County's sheriff.

Another type of ballad called the *corrido* emerged in Mexico and became popular in Arizona. Corridos often retell legends, stories of the Old West, or love stories.

Mariachi music, which began in Mexico, is popular in Mexican restaurants, at weddings, and at festivals. A mariachi band usually includes a violin, trumpets, and several different sizes of guitars.

Many well-known musicians have lived in Arizona. The great Charles Mingus, a jazz bassist and composer, was born in Nogales. Lalo Guerrero, born in Tucson, was a singer, guitarist, and activist. His style greatly influenced many of today's Latino musicians. He was friends with Gilbert Ronstadt, whose daughter Linda has recorded pop tunes, American standards, and Mexican ballads. Marty Robbins, a country and western artist, produced six top 10 tunes during his career, including an album of gunfighter ballads. Arizona has also produced rappers, such as Young Hot Rod and DJ Z-Trip. In recent years, Arizona has experienced a boom in local punk and metal bands. Country music star Dierks Bentley, from Phoenix, and singer-songwriter Michelle Branch, from Sedona, are top-selling recording artists.

For people who prefer classical music, both Phoenix and Tucson have symphony orchestras. The Tucson Symphony Orchestra encourages kids to explore the world of classical music through its programs for young musicians. As part of the Phoenix Symphony's 60th anniversary in 2008, the orchestra presented the world premier of *Enemy Slayer: A Navajo Oratorio*, a piece that represents the Native American presence in the state. Phoenix composer Mark Grey wrote the music, and Navajo writer Laura Tohe, a professor at Arizona State University, wrote the words.

MINI-BIO

CHARLES MINGUS: JAZZ MUSICIAN

Charles Mingus (1922–1979) was born in Nogales. He began learning music while attending church and by listening to the radio. In the 1950s, he moved to New York and became friends with leading jazz musicians of the time, including Charlie Parker, Miles Davis, and Duke Ellington. Mingus became a top bass player and bandleader. He also was a noted composer whose works emphasized originality and improvisation. In the mid-1970s, Mingus contracted ALS, or Lou Gehrig's disease, which confined him to a wheelchair. He continued to compose music by singing into a tape recorder.

❓ **Want to know more?** Visit www.factsfornow.scholastic.com and enter the keyword **Arizona**.

WORDS TO KNOW

improvisation *the act of composing or playing without preparation*

oratorio *a musical composition for voices and instruments, often with a religious theme*

Author Zane Grey had a cabin in Arizona and set many of his novels in the state.

LITERATURE

Stories of the Old West have poured from the pens of Arizona writers. Zane Grey wrote dozens of Western novels, including *Riders of the Purple Sage*. Alan Dean Foster's work includes science-fiction novels, Westerns, and historical works.

Many Arizonans have written works for children. Marianne Mitchell writes novels for middle-grade students. Her mysteries *Finding Zola* and *Firebug* are both set in Arizona. Conrad Storad is a nonfiction author who has written Arizona-based books such as *Sonoran Desert A to Z* and *Flying Colors: Beautiful Birds of the Southwest*. Another Arizonan, Joan Ganz Cooney, created stories for children, but on television rather than in books. She is the cofounder of the Children's Television Workshop, which produces *Sesame Street*.

SPORTS

In Arizona, many people take advantage of the great weather and enjoy outdoor activities. People hike, bike, swim, and golf all year long—although during the summer many get their exercise in the early hours, before the temperature rises. Friday night high school football games draw big crowds. College games on the weekends draw fans to cheer for the Arizona State University Sun Devils or the University of Arizona Wildcats.

Both schools have produced professional athletes. Champion golfer Phil Mickelson fine-tuned his form at Arizona State University, as did Annika Sörenstam, one of the most successful female golfers in history. Lorena Ochoa, another golf legend, attended the University of Arizona. Baseball's Reggie Jackson and Barry Bonds played for the Sun Devils, while the Wildcats turned out National Basketball Association stars such as Damon Stoudamire and Michael Dickerson.

MINI-BIO

STEPHENIE MEYER: VAMPIRE NOVELIST

If you're a fan of horror books and movies, you'll be glad to meet Stephenie Meyer (1973–), the creator of the vampire series Twilight. Born in Connecticut, Meyer grew up in Phoenix and attended high school in Scottsdale. The idea for Twilight came to her in a dream about a human girl and a vampire who was in love with the girl. Meyer began writing a story based on her dream, and in three months, she completed her first Twilight novel. Since then, her four Twilight novels have been translated into 37 different languages, with more than 100 million copies sold worldwide.

Want to know more? Visit www.factsfornow.scholastic.com and enter the keyword **Arizona**.

MAJOR LEAGUE BALL—AT A DISCOUNT

During spring training, teams participate in Arizona's Cactus League. Early in February, baseball players for a dozen Major League Baseball teams head to Arizona, where they get in shape and play baseball. Tickets are cheap, but the baseball is truly major league.

MINI-BIO

REGGIE JACKSON: HALL OF FAME SLUGGER

Reggie Jackson (1946–) is one of baseball's all-time greatest power hitters. Born in Pennsylvania, Jackson attended Arizona State University on a football scholarship. In 21 seasons as a big-league ballplayer, Jackson slugged 583 home runs and won five World Series championships. One of his most memorable moments came when he hit three consecutive home runs in the final game of the 1978 World Series. Jackson was elected to the Baseball Hall of Fame in 1993.

? **Want to know more?** Visit www.factsfornow .scholastic.com and enter the keyword **Arizona**.

Professional sports fans cheer for the Arizona Cardinals of the National Football League, the Phoenix Suns of the National Basketball Association, the Phoenix Mercury of the Women's National Basketball Association, and the Arizona Diamondbacks of Major League Baseball. The Diamondbacks, a team founded in 1998, shocked the baseball world by winning the World Series in 2001. Never before had such a young team won the World Series championship.

Fans and players stand for the national anthem before the Arizona Diamondbacks take on the Colorado Rockies.

A bronco and rider at the annual Prescott Frontier Days rodeo

Arizona would not be true to its heritage if it did not have an active rodeo circuit. Cowboys have been in Arizona since the early days of Spanish and Mexican settlement. Today's rodeos test a cowboy's or cowgirl's skills at riding, roping, and mastering cattle. There is a high school rodeo league, which trains young riders to compete. Riders from throughout the West compete in the Prescott Frontier Days, the oldest rodeo in the world. In Tucson, La Fiesta de Los Vaqueros has been held for more than 80 years. It is one of the top professional rodeos in North America.

86

READ ABOUT

U.S. senator John McCain talks with Arizona residents at a town hall meeting in Phoenix.

CHAPTER SEVEN

GOVERNMENT

★

ARIZONA IS AMONG THE FASTEST-GROWING STATES IN THE NATION. The growing population needs schools to attend and clean water to drink. They need well-maintained roads and enough fire-fighters and police officers to keep them safe. They want their garbage to be picked up, and they want well-supplied public libraries. It is the government's job to supply these services.

ARIZONA'S CONSTITUTION

Arizona's government is based on its original constitution, which was approved in 1912 when Arizona became a state. An important feature of the constitution is the Declaration of Rights, which guarantees rights such as a speedy trial and the right to privacy.

Under the Arizona Constitution, the state government has three branches: executive, legislative, and judicial. The governor, cabinet, and departments make up the executive branch. The senate and house of representatives make up the legislature. The judicial branch

The state capitol in Phoenix

Capital City

This map shows places of interest in Phoenix, Arizona's capital city.

includes the justices, judges, courts, prisons, and jails. The three branches work together to ensure the rights of Arizona's citizens.

THE EXECUTIVE BRANCH

The executive branch is in charge of carrying out the laws. The governor is the head of the executive branch. Arizonans expect the governor to be a leader who can work through problems. The governor signs bills into law and can appoint and dismiss heads of many executive departments. He or she also appoints judges to the state supreme court and the court of appeals, although after a two-year term, the judges must run for election to keep their jobs.

Capitol Facts

Here are some fascinating facts about Arizona's state capitol.

Designed by: James Riley Gordon
Built: 1899–1900
Dome: Copper-covered, topped with a statue called *Winged Victory*
Building materials: Malapai, granite, copper

Governor Jan Brewer signs a health care bill into law in 2013.

Q8 WHO ARE THE FAB FIVE?

A8 In November 1997, five Arizona women were elected to the five top jobs in the state. Jane Dee Hull became the state's first elected female governor. Betsy Bayless became secretary of state. Janet Napolitano, who later became governor, was elected attorney general. Carol Springer won the state treasurer's job, and Lisa Keegan became superintendent of public instruction. Although these women do not hold their original Arizona government jobs anymore, they are still very influential within the state.

Arizona's governor must be at least 25 years old, have lived in Arizona for five years, and have been a citizen of the United States for at least 10 years. Governors hold office for four years and may serve only two terms in a row. As of 2014, Arizona was the only state in the Union to have had four female governors.

Arizonans elect 10 other executive branch officials. They include the secretary of state, who oversees elections; the treasurer, who is in charge of the state's money; and the attorney general, who represents the state in court. The executive branch also includes many different departments, such as the Agriculture Department, the Parks Department, and the Education Department.

Arizona State Government

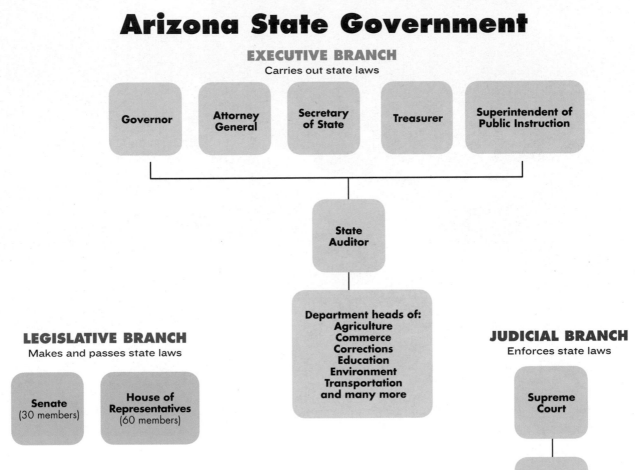

EXECUTIVE BRANCH
Carries out state laws

Governor | Attorney General | Secretary of State | Treasurer | Superintendent of Public Instruction

State Auditor

Department heads of:
Agriculture
Commerce
Corrections
Education
Environment
Transportation
and many more

LEGISLATIVE BRANCH
Makes and passes state laws

Senate (30 members) | House of Representatives (60 members)

JUDICIAL BRANCH
Enforces state laws

Supreme Court
Court of Appeals (2 divisions)
Superior Courts (9 divisions)
Municipal Courts

THE LEGISLATIVE BRANCH

The Arizona legislature is made up of a senate and a house of representatives. The senate has 30 senators, and the house has 60 representatives.

Senators serve two-year terms and are permitted to serve only four terms, for a total of eight years. One of its members serves as the president and leads the senate. The senate president appoints senators to committees, such as finance, education, or health. Senators generally serve on several committees, and the senator who has been on the committee the longest is the chairperson.

The Arizona House of Representatives discusses the state budget in 2011.

Representing Arizona

This list shows the number of elected officials who represent Arizona, both on the state and national levels.

OFFICE	NUMBER	LENGTH OF TERM
State senators	30	2 years
State representatives	60	2 years
U.S. senators	2	6 years
U.S. representatives	9	2 years
Presidential electors	11	—

Members of the Arizona house of representatives also serve two-year terms and are limited to a total of four terms, or eight years. The speaker of the house is the leader who appoints representatives to committees, calls on people to speak, and sets the agenda, or schedule, for discussion.

The legislature proposes, studies, and passes bills that may eventually become laws. Once a bill is passed, the governor either signs it into law or vetoes (rejects) it. The legislature can override the governor's veto by voting again and passing the bill into law with a two-thirds vote.

THE JUDICIAL BRANCH

The judicial branch consists of the state's court system. The highest court is the Arizona Supreme Court, followed by superior courts and the court of appeals. The state court system handles both criminal and civil cases. In criminal cases, the state attorney general's office tries people accused of committing crimes such as murder or theft. In civil cases, one person who feels injured in some way by another files a lawsuit asking for payment for damages.

The court system works in steps. Arizona has 180 courts, ranging from lower courts to the supreme court. The lowest courts in Arizona are municipal (city) courts, where judges hear cases on matters such as traffic violations, shoplifting, and disturbing the peace.

Cases involving more serious crimes are brought before the higher courts. Superior courts handle the more serious criminal and civil cases.

If someone believes the court made a mistake during a trial, he or she can ask the court of appeals to review the decision. Decisions made by the court of appeals can be reviewed by the state supreme court, which has five justices.

In Arizona, the voters elect some judges, while the governor appoints others. For the supreme court and the

MINI-BIO

SANDRA DAY O'CONNOR: SUPREME COURT JUSTICE

Sandra Day O'Connor (1930—) grew up on a cattle ranch near the town of Duncan in southeastern Arizona. She went to law school at Stanford University. In 1952, she graduated near the top of her class, but the only job she was offered was as a legal secretary, because at the time it was rare for women to be lawyers. Eventually, she was hired as a **prosecutor** in Arizona. In time, she became a state senator and then a judge. In 1981, President Ronald Reagan nominated her to serve as the first woman on the U.S. Supreme Court. O'Connor, who was highly respected by the Court for her seriousness and independence, retired in 2006.

? Want to know more? Visit www.factsfornow.scholastic.com and enter the keyword **Arizona**.

WORD TO KNOW

prosecutor *a lawyer who works for the government and tries people accused of crimes*

Arizona Counties

This map shows the 15 counties in Arizona. Phoenix, the state capital, is indicated with a star.

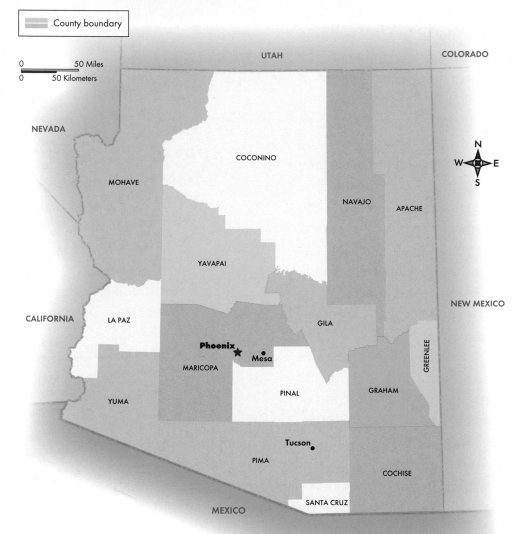

court of appeals, a committee reviews possible candidates. The governor reviews the name suggested by the committee and appoints a candidate to the office. From that time on, that justice or judge must run for election to keep the job. An appointment lasts only two years, but elected terms after that run six years.

NATIVE AMERICAN GOVERNMENTS

Native American reservations are considered independent governments. Most Native American nations have elected leaders, a system for making and enforcing laws, and a justice system. On the reservation, Native Americans follow the laws set by their tribe. Off the reservations, they must follow state laws.

A tribal council governs the Navajo Nation. A president and vice president head the council, which has 24 elected members. The Navajo elect tribal officers every four years.

Navajo Nation leaders meeting in the tribal council chambers in Window Rock in 2006

MINI-BIO

ANNIE DODGE WAUNEKA: NAVAJO LEADER

Annie Dodge Wauneka (1910–1997) was born in Arizona on the Navajo Reservation. Her father, the chairman of the Navajo Tribal Council, made sure she got a good education and understood politics. Wauneka followed in her father's footsteps, and in 1951 she was elected to the council. She was reelected twice, serving three terms. During her career, Wauneka dealt with issues such as schools and housing, but health care was her main concern. She worked tirelessly to make sure that Navajos had access to the best medical care. For her efforts, she was awarded the Presidential Medal of Freedom in 1963.

? Want to know more? Visit www.factsfornow .scholastic.com and enter the keyword **Arizona**.

The reservation is divided into districts, or chapters. Every community has a chapter house, which is the center for the local government. Like state and federal governments, the Navajo government oversees schools, laws, and community affairs. The Navajo Nation has its own police, fire, and rescue services and an office that collects taxes. The Navajo Department of Forestry and Resources promotes environmental awareness and conservation. The Navajo government also provides health services free of charge.

The Navajo Nation has its own judicial system, which includes its own supreme court, family and district courts, and peacemakers. Peacemakers are not police officers. Instead, they are people who help resolve disputes and disagreements within the tribe. Navajos have been using the peacemaker system for more than 500 years.

The Apache people are divided into smaller units, so that White Mountain Apaches and San Carlos Apaches, for example, have separate governments. A tribal chairperson, whom tribal members elect to a four-year term, heads the White Mountain Apache government. The government includes a tribal council that represents the people and makes laws. The San Carlos Apache government includes a chairperson, a vice chairperson, and a tribal council.

Joe Shirley Jr. (left) of the Navajo Nation shakes hands with Todd Honyaoma Sr. (right) of the Hopi Nation after signing a cooperative agreement in 2006.

Traditionally, every Hopi village has its own government made up of a chief and the chief's advisers. That is because Hopis consider every group or community a separate nation. According to Hopi law, each village should be able to deal with outside governments on its own. But the federal government would rather deal with the Hopi people as one unit, so in 1936 the Hopi Nation formed a tribal government. As with the Navajo Nation, the Hopi people are a **sovereign** nation, and they make their own laws.

WORD TO KNOW

sovereign *independent; under its own government*

State Flag

Thirteen alternating rays of red and gold fill the top half of the Arizona flag. The rays represent both the rays of the setting sun and the original 13 colonies that formed the United States. The bottom half of the flag is a field of blue that is the same shade as is found on the U.S. flag. Proud of its rank as the nation's largest producer of copper, Arizona placed a copper-colored star in the flag's center. The Arizona state flag was officially adopted on February 17, 1917.

State Seal

The Arizona state seal is a circle with a shield in the center. The shield depicts the state's landscape and important resources. In the background is a mountain range with the sun rising behind the peaks. Near the mountains are a lake and a dam. Irrigated fields, orchards, and cattle fill the center of the shield, while in the foreground is a miner with a pick and shovel. Above the picture is the state motto, *Ditat Deus*, meaning "God enriches." The words "Great Seal of the State of Arizona" and "1912," the year Arizona was admitted to the United States, surround the seal in a copper-colored circle.

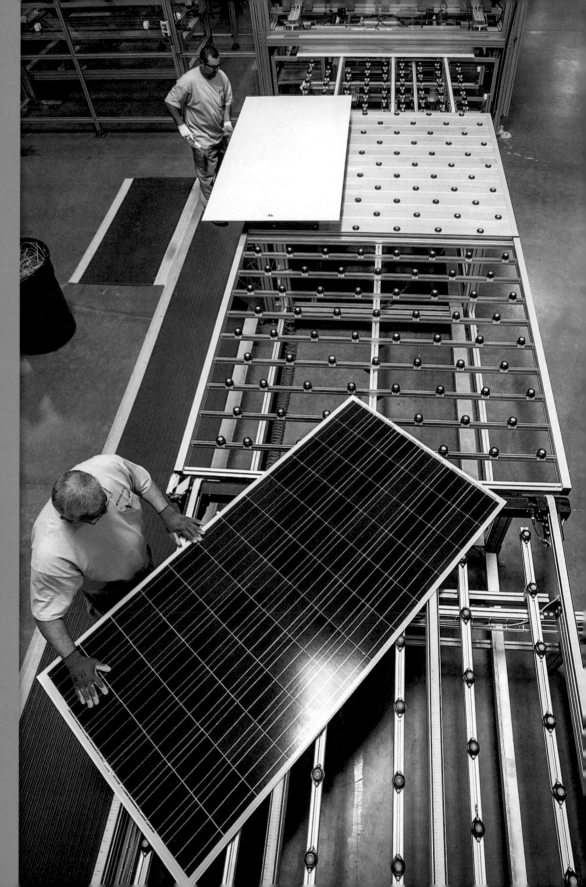

READ ABOUT

Workers inspect their products at a solar panel manufacturer in Goodyear.

CHAPTER EIGHT

ECONOMY

★

HUNDREDS OF YEARS BEFORE EUROPEAN SETTLERS ARRIVED IN ARIZONA, NATIVE PEOPLE FARMED THE LAND AND DUG SILVER AND COPPER FROM THE EARTH. The state has grown dramatically in the past 500 years, but farmers still plant crops and miners still remove copper from the ground. Today, however, you're more likely to find Arizonans building computers or working in banks. Farmers, miners, factory workers, businesspeople—they all contribute to the state's economy.

A worker harvests lettuce at Crooked Sky Farms in Phoenix.

Arizona grows enough cotton each year to provide more than one pair of jeans for every American.

AGRICULTURE

Arizona's agriculture is fairly evenly balanced between crops and livestock. The industry produces $9.2 billion for the state every year. Crops account for 53 percent of this, while the remaining 47 percent is livestock and livestock products.

The state's most valuable crop is lettuce, which makes up 14 percent of Arizona's total crop production. Yuma is a center of winter lettuce production. Other food crops include citrus fruits, honeydew melons, cantaloupes, and potatoes. Greenhouse and nursery products (trees, shrubs, flowers, and garden seedlings) are also big sellers. Arizona ranks eighth in the nation in cotton production and also produces large amounts of wheat, barley, and hay.

Because the state receives so little rain, fields are irrigated. The cost of water adds to the cost of producing crops. The state's major livestock products are cattle, calves, and dairy products. The state has about one million head of cattle and produces 386 million pounds (175 million kg) of beef yearly.

Arizona has 1.6 million egg-laying hens, which produce more than 5.8 billion eggs yearly. Arizonans also raise large numbers of hogs, sheep, and lambs. The state's roughly 186,000 milk cows produce more than 2.17 million tons (1.97 metric tons) of milk each year.

The average milking cow in Arizona produces 2,763 gallons (10,459 liters) of milk each year.

MANUFACTURING INDUSTRY

Manufacturing accounts for 9.6 percent of the state's economy. The state's largest manufacturing industry produces computers and electronics. Arizonans process cotton into cloth, crops into food, and trees into lumber. They spin wool from sheep to make yarn and weave it into cloth. Arizonans also produce transportation equipment, metal goods, machinery, printed goods, and furniture.

Many of the goods manufactured in Arizona are exported. More than 50 percent of Arizona's exports go to Mexico, Canada, and China. Other large markets are Japan and the United Kingdom.

Top Products

Agriculture Cattle, calves, dairy products, cotton, lettuce, hay, cauliflower, cantaloupes, broccoli, sorghum, barley, potatoes

Manufacturing Computer and electronic equipment, cotton cloth, communications systems, transportation equipment, processed foods, chemicals, printing and publishing, sheet metal, windows and door frames, machinery

Mining Copper, molybdenum, gold, silver, coal, sand and gravel, crushed stone

ARIZONA MINING AND
MINERAL MUSEUM

Mining has played a major role in the history of Arizona. This history is told at the Arizona Mining and Mineral Museum, which is located in Phoenix. The museum's exhibits attract people interested in mining—and those who love beautiful rocks. On display are more than 3,000 minerals, along with meteorites, turquoise, raw ore samples, and "moon rocks," which astronauts brought back from the moon. The museum also displays historic mining equipment and railcars used in mines.

Major Agricultural and Mining Products

This map shows where Arizona's major agricultural and mining products come from. See a cow? That means cattle are raised there.

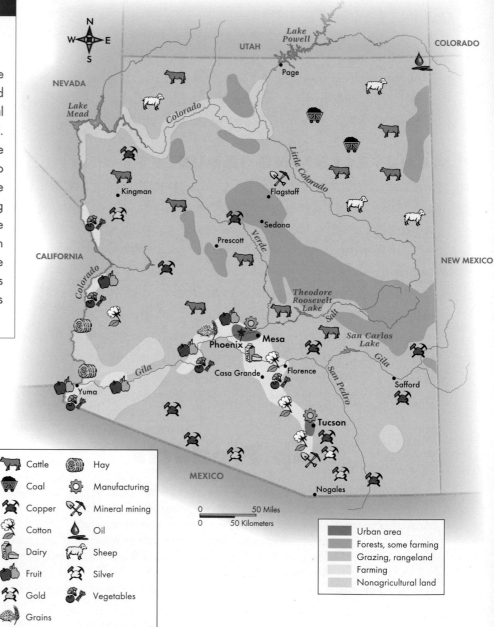

MINING

Copper mining is the major mining industry in Arizona. In 2011, the state produced more than $4.6 billion worth of copper. The largest active mine is in Morenci. It produces roughly 840 million pounds (381 million kg) of copper each year, more than half the state's total copper production.

While copper is the mineral that's most valuable to the state's economy, Arizona also produces other precious metals and gemstones. Gold, silver, molybdenum, and uranium mines are highly productive.

Arizona is the leading gemstone-mining state in the country. Peridot is mined at Peridot Mesa, which has one of the largest deposits of this vivid green gem. Purple amethyst comes from the Four Peaks mine near Phoenix. Turquoise is found in many places throughout the state and is often combined with Arizona silver to make stunning jewelry.

SERVICE INDUSTRIES

Today, services are the largest part of Arizona's economy. The government employs many service workers. Schoolteachers, police officers, and people who repair roads are all service workers.

FAQ

Q: WHAT IS COPPER USED FOR?

A: Copper is used in telephone wires, keys, doorknobs, pipes, refrigerators, and computers. The average household contains 400 pounds (181 kg) of copper, while a car has about 50 pounds (23 kg) of it. About 50,000 tons of Arizona copper is used to make coins each year.

MINI-BIO

ARTURO MORENO: SELF-MADE BILLIONAIRE

Arturo Moreno (1946–) grew up in Tucson, the oldest of 11 children. He graduated from the University of Arizona in 1973 and began working for a company that sold billboard advertising. After seven years, he went to work for Outdoor Systems, another billboard company, soon becoming its president. Under his leadership, Outdoor Systems grew to be the nation's largest billboard company. When the company was sold in 1999, Moreno became a billionaire. In 2003, he made history when he bought the Anaheim Angels baseball team, becoming the first Hispanic owner of a major sports team in the United States.

? Want to know more? Visit www.factsfornow.scholastic.com and enter the keyword **Arizona**.

A park ranger gives a talk to students at Grand Canyon National Park.

EMMETT CHAPPELLE: SCIENTIST

Emmett Chappelle (1925—), a native of Phoenix, is a bio-chemist who worked for many years with the National Aeronautics and Space Administration (NASA). While at NASA, he discovered that a specific combination of chemicals causes all living things to emit light. Chappelle has been recog-nized as one of the most distinguished African American scientists of the 20th century and was inducted into the National Inventors Hall of Fame in 2007.

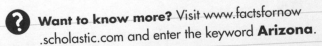

? Want to know more? Visit www.factsfornow .scholastic.com and enter the keyword **Arizona**.

Arizona attracts millions of tourists each year. They play golf, hike in national parks, or visit museums. They eat in res-taurants, stay in hotels, and shop in stores. The people who work in the parks, museums, hotels, and stores are working in the service industry.

Real estate agents, bankers, and scientists in laboratories also provide services. So do gas sta-tion attendants, doctors, and the person who delivers your pizza. In fact, more than half of all jobs in Arizona today are in the service industry. And they all contribute to Arizona's growing economy.

What Do Arizonans Do?

This color-coded chart shows what industries Arizonans work in.

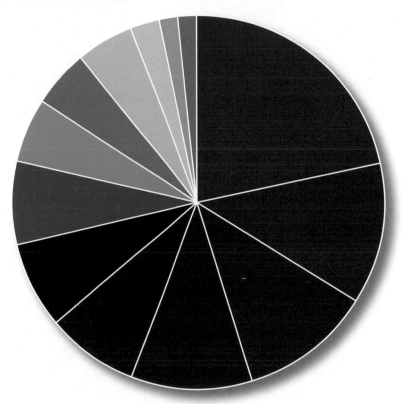

21.1% Educational services, health care, and social assistance, 537,833

12.2% Retail trade, 334,731

11.3% Professional, scientific, management, administrative, and waste management services, 308,451

10.5% Arts, entertainment, recreation, accommodation, and food services, 287,966

8.0% Construction, 220,465

8.0% Finance, insurance, real estate, rental, and leasing, 220,282

7.6% Manufacturing, 208,723

5.6% Public administration, 154,706

4.9% Transportation, warehousing, and utilities, 135,163

4.8% Other services, except public administration, 130,869

2.6% Wholesale trade, 70,702

1.8% Information, 50,421

1.4% Agriculture, forestry, fishing, hunting, and mining, 38,765

Source: U.S. Census Bureau, 2010 census

CHAPTER NINE

TRAVEL
GUIDE

TRAVEL GUIDE

★

NOW THAT YOU KNOW ABOUT ARIZONA, LET'S TAKE A TOUR OF ALL THERE IS TO SEE. We'll travel through the Grand Canyon, down the Colorado River, and into the Sonoran Desert. We'll explore the cities of Phoenix and Tucson, and then head northeast to the Petrified Forest and Canyon de Chelly. Get your map, and we'll be on our way!

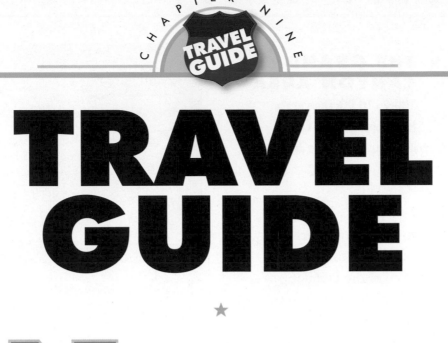

← Follow along with this travel map. We'll begin in Williams and travel all the way to Holbrook.

THE GRAND CANYON AREA

THINGS TO DO: Gaze at the jaw-dropping Grand Canyon, swim in Lake Powell, or explore caverns deep under the earth.

Williams

★ **Grand Canyon National Park:** The Colorado River carved this massive canyon, one of the wonders of the natural world, millions of years ago. Most visitors see the ribbons of red and brown rock only from the canyon rim, but for a different view, hike down into the canyon.

Peach Springs

★ **Grand Canyon Caverns:** First, you go down about 21 stories into the ground—that's 210 feet (64 m). Then you trek among rock formations that look like they came from the moon. It's deep, it's dark, it's dramatic.

Page

★ **Glen Canyon National Recreation Area:** In the middle of the desert, Lake Powell's blue waters in Glen Canyon are a welcome invitation. Enjoy the rosy sand beaches, the gentle rolling rocks, and the spectacular canyons.

Sandstone patterns at Vermilion Cliffs National Monument

★ **Vermilion Cliffs National Monument:** Located in the Paria Canyon-Vermilion Cliffs Wilderness area, this desert is home to bighorn sheep, pronghorns, and birds of prey.

THE WEST

THINGS TO DO: Learn about Native American pottery, visit a Wild West jail, or see London Bridge . . . yes, the London Bridge from England!

Kingman

★ **Route 66 Museum:** In the 1950s, many people traveling across the country took Route 66, a road that went from Chicago to Los Angeles. This museum takes visitors back to the days when teens gathered in the soda shop and danced to the new music called rock 'n' roll blaring from the jukebox.

* **Mohave Museum of History and Arts:** This small museum is dedicated to the history of Arizona and its Native people. In the Hualapai Native American room, you'll find a full-size hut along with pottery, baskets, and other Native crafts.

Lake Havasu City

* **London Bridge:** For those who want a bit of old England in the middle of the Arizona desert, visit London Bridge. A re-created English village adds to the atmosphere.
* **Havasu National Wildlife Refuge:** Put on a life jacket and take a canoe ride along Topock Gorge. You'll spot hundreds of birds in their natural environment. Inspect the ancient petroglyphs that cover Picture Rock. And watch for daring bighorn sheep that travel the gorge's cliffs.

Canoeing at Havasu National Wildlife Refuge

Q8 HOW DID LONDON BRIDGE WIND UP IN ARIZONA?

A8 In 1958, developer Robert McCulloch spotted Lake Havasu from a plane and decided to build a community in the area. McCulloch wanted his community to be unique, so he brought an unusual tourist attraction, London Bridge. The bridge was slowly sinking into the River Thames in London, England, and the British were happy to sell it to McCulloch. London Bridge arrived in Arizona in more than 10,000 pieces. It was reassembled and has been a tourist attraction ever since.

Yuma

* **Betty's Kitchen:** Don't let the name fool you because Betty's Kitchen is not a restaurant. It's not even a kitchen. It is a shady spot in the Sonoran Desert that is ideal for picnics, hiking, bird-watching, and fishing.
* **Yuma Territorial Prison:** Relive the days when bank robbers terrorized towns, and no one felt safe. The prison museum tells the tales of the lawbreakers. More than 3,000 prisoners, including 29 women, lived in Yuma Prison during its 33 years of operation.

AROUND TUCSON

THINGS TO DO: Hike in the desert, grind mesquite beans, or watch two gunfighters shoot it out.

Tucson

★ **Saguaro National Park:** This park is dedicated to a cactus, and rightly so. The saguaro provides food and shelter for countless desert animals. Majestic saguaros grow as high as 75 feet (23 m) in this park.

★ **Arizona-Sonora Desert Museum:** Just west of Tucson is this museum dedicated to desert life. It is a combination of history museum, garden, and zoo. Desert birds, reptiles, and mammals live in natural habitats. Cat Canyon—where cougars, ocelots, margays, coatimundis, and jaguarundis can be seen up close—is a favorite site.

A guide holds a barn owl at the Arizona-Sonora Desert Museum.

★ **Tucson Botanical Gardens:** Cacti and their flowers play a leading role at this garden. Besides exploring a variety of gardens, you can learn about how the Tohono O'odham traditionally used plants. You can even try your hand at grinding mesquite beans.

★ **Barrio Historico:** This old part of Tucson features traditional **adobe** buildings.

WORD TO KNOW

adobe *bricks made of sun-dried clay; also, a house made with these bricks*

★ **Buckelew Farm Pumpkin Festival and Corn Maze:** Open only in late fall, this farm offers horse-drawn wagon rides, a pick-your-own pumpkin field, and a maze cut into a cornfield.

★ **Funtasticks Family Fun Park:** This place is designed with kids in mind. It has a miniature golf course, bumper boats, a batting cage, and an arcade.

★ **Children's Museum Tucson:** This is one museum where everything is hands-on rather than hands-off. First you can check out a submarine, and then you can try to find your way out of a maze.

A touring stagecoach in Tombstone

TOMBSTONE EPITAPHS

Someone in Tombstone must have had a sense of humor. Read what was carved on Lester Moore's tombstone:

HERE LIES
LESTER MOORE
FOUR SLUGS
FROM A 44
NO LES
NO MORE

★ **Mission San Xavier del Bac:** This mission is one of the few buildings remaining from the time when Spain ruled Arizona.

★ **Old Tucson:** See where movie history was made. This was the location for shooting classic Westerns such as *Gunfight at the O.K. Corral*, *Three Amigos*, and *Tombstone*. In 1995, the studio burned down, but it has been rebuilt.

Tombstone

★ **Boothill Graveyard:** It is not often that a visit to a graveyard is a recommended tourist activity, but don't miss Boothill. The **epitaphs** on the tombstones make the trip worthwhile.

WORD TO KNOW

epitaphs *writings in memory of dead people, often on tombstones*

★ **Touring the Town:** Walk the streets that the Earp brothers once walked. Stop by the Wyatt Earp House and the Tombstone Courthouse. And don't miss the daily gunfights at the O.K. Corral.

CENTRAL ARIZONA

THINGS TO DO: Catch a ball game, take a picture of Camelback Mountain, or head for the stars.

Phoenix

★ **Phoenix Art Museum:** You will see lots of extraordinary art at the Phoenix Art Museum. On Saturdays and Sundays, kids can attend events where they might learn how to make art prints or celebrate the music of Mexico.

- **Heard Museum:** The Heard Museum has one of the best Native American arts and crafts collections found anywhere. Exhibits range from a collection of Native American footwear to video and art by young Navajo artist Steven Yazzie.

- **Arizona Science Center:** At this hands-on museum, visitors can explore more than 350 exhibits. You might take off for outer space at the planetarium, investigate the king-size ant farm, or play a virtual reality game that puts you in the middle of the action.

Goldfield

- **Ghost Town:** If you find the Old West fascinating, head to Goldfield, an authentic ghost town. You can even tour the gold mine that made the town boom for a time.

A Hohokam structure, protected by a canopy, at Casa Grande Ruins National Monument

Mesa

- **Salt River Tubing:** Arizona is hot, but traveling down the Salt River on a tube is hot stuff! Float along for anywhere from 1½ hours to 4 hours. It is wet, wild, and refreshing.

Scottsdale

- **African American Multicultural Museum:** This museum features art, historical objects, and more from the people of many different backgrounds who built Arizona.

Casa Grande

- **Casa Grande Ruins National Monument:** This site preserves an ancient Hohokam village. Casa Grande Ruins was the nation's first archaeological preserve. The site protects the heritage of a culture that lived more than 1,000 years ago.

Sedona

- **Tlaquepaque Arts & Crafts Village:** Shoppers get ready, because you are heading to one of the oldest markets in the Southwest. Shop, put your feet up by a fountain, or admire the art in a gallery.

- **Slide Rock State Park:** Nature made this waterslide of stone, and it is a favorite with kids.

Flagstaff

★ **San Francisco Peaks:** Come visit the mountains that the Navajo, Hopi, and Havasupai peoples consider sacred. Many people travel here to hike and see wildlife.

★ **Sunset Crater Volcano National Monument:** When you walk on the lava flow trails at this park, you'll feel like you've landed on another planet.

Tonto

★ **Tonto National Monument:** Explore the ruins of two cliff dwellings established by Native people in about 1300. The homes were built high on a steep hillside in well-protected natural caves.

THE EAST

THINGS TO DO: Learn about dinosaurs, visit ancient Hopi villages, and view the spectacular landscapes of the Painted Desert.

Chinle

★ **Hopi Reservation:** The Hopi villages lie atop three spectacular mesas. Old Oraibi is perhaps the oldest continuously inhabited community in North America, dating back to about 1100.

FAQ

Q: WHO IS GERTIE?

A: In 1985, scientists discovered the bones of a dinosaur that was a smaller relative of the huge *Tyrannosaurus*. The bones lay among the fallen trees of the Petrified Forest. Gertie, as the dinosaur was named, has been tentatively identified as a *Staurikosaur*. In life, Gertie was a meat-eating creature that measured 7 to 8 feet (2 to 2.4 m) long and weighed about 150 pounds (68 kg).

★ **Monument Valley:** On the border of Utah and Arizona, Monument Valley is filled with sandy desert, red buttes, and beautiful scenery.

★ **Painted Desert:** The Painted Desert is not truly painted. Instead, it is a region of multicolored, eroded rock formations.

Holbrook

★ **Petrified Forest National Park:** You'll see piles of colorful petrified wood at this park. You can also learn about dinosaurs and see the fossils of a creature named Gertie.

A petrified log at Petrified Forest National Park

WRITING PROJECTS

Check out these ideas for creating a campaign brochure and writing you-are-there narratives. Or research famous people from Arizona.

118

ART PROJECTS

You can illustrate the state song, create a dazzling PowerPoint presentation, or learn about the state quarter and design your own.

119

TIMELINE

What happened when? This timeline highlights important events in the state's history—and shows what was happening throughout the United States at the same time.

122

GLOSSARY

Remember the Words to Know from the chapters in this book? They're all collected here.

125

FAST FACTS

Use this section to find fascinating facts about state symbols, land area and population statistics, weather, sports teams, and much more.

126

SCIENCE, TECHNOLOGY, ENGINEERING, & MATH PROJECTS

120

Make weather maps, graph population statistics, and research endangered species that live in the state.

PRIMARY VS. SECONDARY SOURCES

121

So what are primary and secondary sources? And what's the diff? This section explains all that and where you can find them.

BIOGRAPHICAL DICTIONARY

133

This at-a-glance guide highlights some of the state's most important and influential people. Visit this section and read about their contributions to the state, the country, and the world.

RESOURCES

Books and much more. Take a look at these additional sources for information about the state.

138

WRITING PROJECTS

Write a Memoir, Journal, or Editorial for Your School Newspaper!

Picture Yourself . . .

★ As a Navajo teenager preparing to go on a journey. Describe the Blessingway ceremony that will guide you on a safe path.
   SEE: Chapter Two, pages 32–33.

★ Living in an Arizona mining town. What would life be like on the Arizona frontier? What would your responsibilities be? Describe what comforts of life you would enjoy and which you would miss, and why.
   SEE: Chapter Four, pages 47–49.

Create an Election Brochure or Web Site!

Run for office! Throughout this book, you've read about some of the issues that concern Arizona today. As a candidate for governor of Arizona, create a campaign brochure or Web site.

★ Explain how you meet the qualifications to be governor of Arizona.

★ Talk about the three or four major issues you'll focus on if you're elected.

★ Remember, you'll be responsible for Arizona's budget. How would you spend the taxpayers' money?
   SEE: Chapter Seven, pages 89–90.

Create an interview script with a famous person from Arizona!

★ Research various influential Arizonans, such as Cochise, Arturo Moreno, Sandra Day O'Connor, Charles Mingus, and many others.

★ Based on your research, pick one person you would most like to talk with.

★ Write a script of the interview. What questions would you ask? How would this person answer? Create a question-and-answer format. You may want to supplement this writing project with a voice-recording dramatization of the interview.
   SEE: Chapters Four, Six, Seven, and Eight, pages 51–53, 81, 93, and 105, and the Biographical Dictionary, pages 133–137.

ART PROJECTS

Create a PowerPoint Presentation or Visitors' Guide

Welcome to Arizona!

Arizona's a great place to visit and to live! From its natural beauty to its historical sites, there's plenty to see and do. In your PowerPoint presentation or brochure, highlight 10 to 15 of Arizona's fascinating landmarks. Be sure to include:

★ a map of the state showing where these sites are located

★ photos, illustrations, Web links, natural history facts, geographic stats, climate and weather, plants and wildlife, and recent discoveries

SEE: Chapter Nine, pages 108–115, and Fast Facts, pages 126–127.

Illustrate the Lyrics to the Arizona State Song

("Arizona")

Use markers, paints, photos, collages, colored pencils, or computer graphics to illustrate the lyrics to "Arizona." Turn your illustrations into a picture book, or scan them into PowerPoint and add music.

SEE: The lyrics to "Arizona" on page 128.

Research Arizona's State Quarter

From 1999 to 2008, the U.S. Mint introduced new quarters commemorating each of the 50 states in the order that they were admitted to the Union. Each state's quarter features a unique design on its reverse, or back.

★ Research the significance of the image. Who designed the quarter? Who chose the final design?

★ Design your own Arizona quarter. What images would you choose for the reverse?

★ Make a poster showing the Arizona quarter and label each image.

GO TO: www.factsfornow.scholastic.com. Enter the keyword **Arizona** and look for the link to the Arizona quarter.

SCIENCE, TECHNOLOGY, ENGINEERING, & MATH PROJECTS

Graph Population Statistics!

★ Compare population statistics (such as ethnic background, birth, death, and literacy rates) in Arizona counties or major cities.

★ In your graph or chart, look at population density and write sentences describing what the population statistics show; graph one set of population statistics and write a paragraph explaining what the graphs reveal.

SEE: Chapter Six, pages 70–74.

Create a Weather Map of Arizona!

Use your knowledge of Arizona's geography to research and identify conditions that result in specific weather events. What is it about the geography of Arizona that makes it vulnerable to things such as droughts? Create a weather map or poster that shows the weather patterns over the state. Include a caption explaining the technology used to measure weather phenomena and provide data.

SEE: Chapter One, pages 15–16.

Track Endangered Species

Using your knowledge of Arizona's wildlife, research which animals and plants are endangered or threatened.

★ Find out what the state is doing to protect these species.

★ Chart known populations of the animals and plants, and report on changes in certain geographic areas.

SEE: Chapter One, pages 22–23.

Mexican gray wolf

PRIMARY VS. SECONDARY SOURCES

What's the Diff?

Your teacher may require at least one or two primary sources and one or two secondary sources for your assignment. So, what's the difference between the two?

★ **Primary sources are original.** You are reading the actual words of someone's diary, journal, letter, autobiography, or interview. Primary sources can also be photographs, maps, prints, cartoons, news/film footage, posters, first-person newspaper articles, drawings, musical scores, and recordings. By the way, when you conduct a survey, interview someone, shoot a video, or take photographs to include in a project, you are creating primary sources!

★ **Secondary sources are what you find in encyclopedias, textbooks, articles, biographies, and almanacs.** These are written by a person or group of people who tell about something that happened to someone else. Secondary sources also recount what another person said or did. This book is an example of a secondary source.

Now that you know what primary sources are—where can you find them?

★ **Your school or local library:** Check the library catalog for collections of original writings, government documents, musical scores, and so on. Some of this material may be stored on microfilm.

★ **Historical societies:** These organizations keep historical documents, photographs, and other materials. Staff members can help you find what you are looking for. History museums are also great places to see primary sources firsthand.

★ **The Internet:** There are lots of sites that have primary sources you can download and use in a project or assignment.

TIMELINE

★ ★ ★

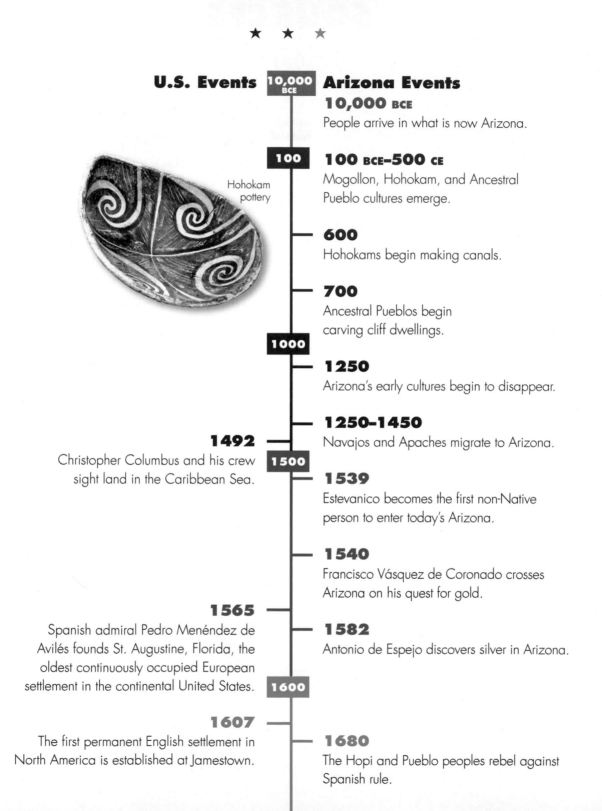

U.S. Events | 10,000 BCE | **Arizona Events**

10,000 BCE
People arrive in what is now Arizona.

100

100 BCE–500 CE
Mogollon, Hohokam, and Ancestral Pueblo cultures emerge.

Hohokam pottery

600
Hohokams begin making canals.

700
Ancestral Pueblos begin carving cliff dwellings.

1000

1250
Arizona's early cultures begin to disappear.

1250–1450
Navajos and Apaches migrate to Arizona.

1492
Christopher Columbus and his crew sight land in the Caribbean Sea.

1500

1539
Estevanico becomes the first non-Native person to enter today's Arizona.

1540
Francisco Vásquez de Coronado crosses Arizona on his quest for gold.

1565
Spanish admiral Pedro Menéndez de Avilés founds St. Augustine, Florida, the oldest continuously occupied European settlement in the continental United States.

1582
Antonio de Espejo discovers silver in Arizona.

1600

1607
The first permanent English settlement in North America is established at Jamestown.

1680
The Hopi and Pueblo peoples rebel against Spanish rule.

U.S. Events

1682

René-Robert Cavelier, Sieur de La Salle, claims more than 1 million square miles (2.6 million sq km) of territory in the Mississippi River basin for France, naming it Louisiana.

1776

Thirteen American colonies declare their independence from Great Britain.

1846–48

The United States fights a war with Mexico over western territories in the Mexican War.

1861–65

The American Civil War is fought between the Northern Union and the Southern Confederacy; it ends with the surrender of the Confederate army, led by General Robert E. Lee.

Cochise

1886

Apache leader Geronimo surrenders to the U.S. Army, ending the last major Native American rebellion against the expansion of the United States into the West.

Arizona Events

1687

Eusebio Kino begins founding missions in Arizona.

1700

1751

Pimas revolt against Spanish rule.

1800

1821

Mexico wins independence from Spain.

1848

The United States takes control of northern Arizona at the end of the Mexican-American War.

1853

With the Gadsden Purchase, the United States buys the final section of today's Arizona.

1859

The first Native American reservation is established in Arizona.

1863

Arizona Territory is established.

1860s–70s

Cochise leads Chiricahua Apaches in a fight against white settlement.

1871

Raiders kill 118 Apaches in the Camp Grant Massacre.

1881

The gunfight at the OK Corral takes place.

1900

1906

Construction begins on the Theodore Roosevelt Dam.

U.S. Events

Arizona Events

1912
Arizona becomes the 48th state.

1917–18
The United States engages in World War I.

1917
Mine owners ship 1,200 striking workers from Bisbee into the desert.

1929
The stock market crashes, plunging the United States more deeply into the Great Depression.

1941–45
The United States engages in World War II.

1942–45
Japanese Americans are confined in internment camps in Arizona.

1950–53
The United States engages in the Korean War.

1950s
Lawsuits challenging discrimination are filed by people of color.

1964–73
The United States engages in the Vietnam War.

1985
Work begins on the Central Arizona Project.

1991
The United States and other nations engage in the brief Persian Gulf War against Iraq.

2000

2001
Terrorists hijack four U.S. aircraft and crash them into the World Trade Center in New York City, the Pentagon in Arlington, Virginia, and a Pennsylvania field, killing thousands.

2001
The Arizona Diamondbacks win the World Series.

2003
The United States and coalition forces invade Iraq.

2010
Arizona passes a strict anti-immigration law.

GLOSSARY

★ ★ ★

adobe bricks made of sun-dried clay; also, a house made with these bricks

archaeology the study of the remains of past human societies

cavalry soldiers who ride on horseback

conquistadores ones who conquer; specifically, leaders in the Spanish conquest of the Americas

conservation the act of saving or preserving something, such as a natural resource, plant, or animal species

defiled dishonored

discrimination unequal treatment based on race, gender, religion, or other factors

ecosystems communities of plants and animals interacting with their environment

epitaphs writings in memory of dead people, often on tombstones

expedition a trip for the purpose of exploration

geometric using straight lines and simple shapes, such as circles or squares

improvisation the act of composing or playing without preparation

internment camps places where people are confined, usually during wartime

masonry made of stone or brick

mesas flat-topped hills

missionaries people who try to convert others to a religion

missions places created by a religious group to spread its beliefs

oratorio a musical composition for voices and instruments, often with a religious theme

plateau an elevated part of the earth with steep slopes

precipitation all water that falls to the earth, including rain, sleet, hail, snow, dew, fog, and mist

prosecutor a lawyer who works for the government and tries people accused of crimes

recalled removed from office

reservation land set aside for Native Americans to live on

reservoirs artificial lakes or tanks created for water storage

segregated separated from others according to race, class, ethnic group, religion, or other factors

sovereign independent; under its own government

strike an organized refusal to work, usually as a sign of protest about working conditions

undocumented lacking documents required for legal immigration or residence

FAST FACTS

★ ★ ★

State Symbols

Statehood date February 14, 1912, the 48th state
Origin of state name Pima Indian word for "small spring" or "place of the small spring," or from a Basque word for "good oak tree"
State capital Phoenix
State nickname Grand Canyon State
State motto *Ditat Deus*, "God enriches"
State bird Coues' cactus wren
State butterfly Arizona butterfly
State flower Saguaro cactus blossom
State fish Arizona, or Apache, trout
State fossil Petrified wood
State gemstone Turquoise
State mammal Ringtail cat
State amphibian Arizona tree frog
State reptile Ridge-nosed rattlesnake
State song "Arizona"
State tree Blue palo verde
State fair Phoenix (late October–early November)

State seal

Geography

Total area; rank 113,998 square miles (295,255 sq km); 6th
Land; rank 113,635 square miles (294,315 sq km); 6th
Water; rank 364 square miles (943 sq km); 48th
Inland water; rank 364 square miles (943 sq km); 42nd
Geographic center Yavapai County, 55 miles (89 km) east to southeast of Prescott
Latitude 31°20' N to 37° N
Longitude 109°3' W to 114°50' W
Highest point Humphreys Peak, 12,633 feet (3,851 m) in Coconino County
Lowest point 70 feet (21 m) at the Colorado River in Yuma County
Longest river Colorado
Largest city Phoenix
Number of counties 15

Population

Population; rank (2010 census)	6,392,017; 15th
Density (2010 census)	56 persons per sq. mi. (22 per sq km)
Population distribution (2010 census)	90% urban, 10% rural
Ethnic distribution (2010 census)	White persons: 57.7%
	Persons of Hispanic or Latino origin: 29.7%
	American Indian and Alaska Native persons: 4.0%
	Black persons: 3.8%
	Asian persons: 2.7%
	Persons reporting two or more races: 1.7%
	Native Hawaiian and other Pacific Islanders: 0.2%
	People of some other race: 0.1%

Weather

Record high temperature	128°F (53°C) at Lake Havasu on June 29, 1994
Record low temperature	−40°F (−40°C) at Hawley Lake near McNary on January 7, 1971
Average July temperature, Phoenix	95°F (35°C)
Average January temperature, Phoenix	56°F (13°C)
Average yearly precipitation, Phoenix	8 inches (20 cm)

State flag

STATE SONG

★ ★ ★

"Arizona"

Margaret R. Clifford wrote the words to the Arizona state song,
and Maurice Blumenthal wrote the music.

Come to this land of sunshine
To this land where life is young.
Where the wide, wide world is waiting,
The songs that will now be sung.
Where the golden sun is flaming
Into warm, white shining day,
And the sons of men are blazing
Their priceless right of way.

Come stand beside the rivers
Within our valley broad.
Stand here with heads uncovered,
In the presence of our God!
While all around, about us
The brave, unconquered band,
As guardians and landmarks
The giant mountains stand.

Not alone for gold and silver
Is Arizona great.
But with graves of heroes sleeping,
All the land is consecrate!
O, come and live beside us
However far ye roam
Come and help us build up temples
And name those temples "home."

Chorus
Sing the song that's in your hearts
Sing of the great Southwest,
Thank God for Arizona
In splendid sunshine dressed.
For thy beauty and thy grandeur,
For thy regal robes so sheen
We hail thee Arizona
Our goddess and our queen.

NATURAL AREAS AND HISTORIC SITES

★ ★ ★

National Parks

Grand Canyon National Park is one of the nation's most visited national parks.

Petrified Forest National Park features petrified wood, rock formations, and the Painted Desert.

Saguaro National Park highlights the tall saguaro cactus, the symbol of the Southwest.

National Recreation Areas

Arizona is home to two national recreation areas: *Glen Canyon National Recreation Area* and *Lake Mead National Recreation Area.*

National Monuments

Arizona boasts 15 national monuments: *Canyon de Chelly National Monument, Casa Grande Ruins National Monument, Chiricahua National Monument, Hohokam Pima National Monument, Montezuma Castle National Monument, Navajo National Monument, Organ Pipe Cactus National Monument, Parashant National Monument, Pipe Spring National Monument, Sunset Crater Volcano National Monument, Tonto National Monument, Tuzigoot National Monument, Vermilion Cliffs National Monument, Walnut Canyon National Monument,* and *Wupatki National Monument.*

National Historic Sites

Fort Bowie National Historic Site was the center of U.S. military operations in the mid- to late 1800s, during the last years of armed Native American resistance to U.S. forces.

Hubbell Trading Post National Historic Site is the oldest continuously operating trading post on the Navajo Reservation.

State Parks and Forests

Arizona maintains 31 state parks and recreation areas, including *Alamo Lake State Park, Dead Horse Ranch State Park, Oracle State Park,* and *Slide Rock State Park.*

SPORTS TEAMS

★ ★ ★

NCAA Teams (Division I)

Arizona State University *Sun Devils*
Northern Arizona University *Lumberjacks*
University of Arizona *Wildcats*

PROFESSIONAL SPORTS TEAMS

★ ★ ★

Major League Baseball

Arizona *Diamondbacks*

National Basketball Association

Phoenix *Suns*

National Football League

Arizona *Cardinals*

National Hockey League

Phoenix *Coyotes*

Women's National Basketball Association

Phoenix *Mercury*

CULTURAL INSTITUTIONS

★ ★ ★

Libraries

The *Arizona Historical Society* (Tucson) and the *Arizona State Library* (Phoenix) have extensive historical collections relating to Arizona's history.

The *Phoenix Public Library* is one of the biggest public library systems in the state.

Museums

The *Arizona-Sonora Desert Museum* (Tucson) features exhibits on desert animals and plants.

The *Arizona State Museum* (Tucson) is rich in exhibits on the geography, archaeology, and anthropology of the American Southwest.

The *Kitt Peak National Observatory* (Tucson), on the Tohono O'odham Reservation, has telescopes mounted on the 6,875-foot (2,096 m) peak.

The *Phoenix Art Museum* has a significant collection of southwestern art and art from around the world.

The *Phoenix Museum of History* tells the story of Phoenix and the Salt River valley beginning with the Hohokam people.

The *Tucson Museum of Art and Historic Block* displays art of the Americas, including pre-Columbian and Spanish colonial paintings and furnishings.

White Mountain Apache Culture Center and Museum (Whiteriver) is a museum dedicated to the Apache Nation and culture.

Performing Arts

The *Arizona Opera* (Phoenix) produces operas and concerts at its locations in Phoenix and Tucson, and offers in-school and touring productions for children and adults of all ages.

The *Phoenix Symphony* offers a wide range of programs each year, including classical music, symphony pops, and chamber music.

Universities and Colleges

In 2011, Arizona had 4 public and 42 private institutions of higher learning.

ANNUAL EVENTS

January–March

Arizona National Livestock Show in Phoenix (January)

Southern Arizona Square and Round Dance Festival in Tucson (January)

Gold Rush Days in Wickenburg (February)

Waterfront Fine Art & Chocolate Festival in Scottsdale (February)

La Fiesta de los Vaqueros Rodeo in Tucson (third week in February)

Sedona International Film Festival & Workshop (February–March)

Arizona Scottish Highland Games in Mesa (March)

April–June

Wyatt Earp Days in Tombstone (May)

July–September

Prescott Frontier Days (first week in July)

Arizona Cowboy Poets Gathering in Prescott (August)

Cool Country Cruise-In & Route 66 Festival in Williams (August)

August Doins Rodeo in Payson (August)

Fiesta Septiembre in Wickenburg (September)

Labor Day Rodeo in Sonoita (September)

Grand Canyon Music Festival (September)

Navajo County Fair Rodeo and Little Buckaroo Rodeo in Holbrook (September)

Navajo Nation Fair in Window Rock (September)

October–December

Anza Days in Tubac (October)

Apache Jii Day in Globe-Miami (October)

Celebraciones de la Gente in Flagstaff (October)

Oktoberfest in Tempe (October)

Arizona State Fair in Phoenix (late October–early November)

London Bridge Days at Lake Havasu City (October–November)

Colorado River Crossing Balloon Festival in Yuma (November)

Festival of Lights in Sedona (December)

Edward Abbey (1927–1989) was an author and environmentalist who worked as a ranger at national parks, including the Organ Pipe Cactus National Monument, on the border of Arizona and Mexico. He strongly supported preserving America's wilderness and believed in curbing modernization in society.

Mary Bernard Aguirre (1844–1906), a native of St. Louis, Missouri, traveled to Arizona by covered wagon and became one of the first teachers in the Tucson public schools. She later taught English history and Spanish at the University of Arizona.

Steve Allen (1921–2000), born in New York City, was a graduate of Arizona State Teachers College. A comedian, actor, music composer, and author, he is best known for creating the concept of the television talk show. Allen was the first host of *The Tonight Show*, which began in 1954 and airs to this day.

Bruce Babbitt See page 23.

Erma Bombeck (1927–1996) lived in Paradise Valley and wrote a humor column about family life for newspapers. Her natural style and wit were so engaging that her writing appeared in 700 newspapers and later in best-selling books.

George Brooks (1926–2007) was a civil rights leader in Phoenix and a member of the Arizona state legislature.

Michael Carbajal (1967–) of Phoenix is a four-time world champion boxer. His nickname is Little Hands of Stone.

Lynda Carter

Lynda Carter (1951–), a native of Phoenix, won the title of Miss World USA in 1972. She went on to star in the television show *Wonder Woman*.

Raúl Héctor Castro (1916–) was born in Mexico and moved to Arizona in 1926. In 1974, he was elected governor of Arizona and later served as U.S. ambassador to Argentina.

Raúl Héctor Castro

134

Emmett Chappelle See page 106.

César Chávez See page 66.

Cochise See page 52.

Francisco Vásquez de Coronado See page 39.

Ted Danson (1947–), who was raised near Flagstaff, is an actor who starred in the television show *Cheers* for 11 years.

Dennis DeConcini (1937–) represented Arizona in the U.S. Senate for more than 20 years. He was born in Tucson.

Andy Devine (1905–1977) was a character actor and sidekick in Westerns such as *Stagecoach* and *The Man Who Shot Liberty Valance*. He was born in Flagstaff.

Wyatt Earp See page 55.

Barbara Eden (1934–) of Tucson is a film and television actress who starred in TV's *I Dream of Jeannie*.

Sean Elliott (1968–) is a retired professional basketball player. He played for the University of Arizona before turning pro. He was born in Tucson.

Sean Elliott

Dolan Ellis (1935–) is Arizona's first and only official state balladeer. He was once a member of the singing group the New Christy Minstrels.

Andre Ethier (1982–) is a star outfielder for baseball's Los Angeles Dodgers. Born in Phoenix, he is a two-time all-star and a winner of a Silver Slugger Award and a Gold Glove Award.

Geronimo See page 51.

Barry Goldwater (1909–1998) served as a U.S. senator from Arizona from 1953 to 1965 and 1969 to 1987. In 1964, he was the Republican candidate for president. He was born in Phoenix.

Barry Goldwater

Zane Grey (1872–1939) wrote stories of the Old West. His novel *Riders of the Purple Sage* was one of the most popular Westerns of all time. His work inspired radio and television shows such as *The Lone Ranger* and *Sergeant Preston of the Yukon*. About 60 of his 90 novels were set in Arizona, many based on the land surrounding his cabin near Payson.

Sharlot Madbrith Hall (1870–1943) moved from Kansas to Arizona Territory in 1882, settling near Prescott with her family. She became a poet, magazine editor, and writer, and in 1909 was appointed territorial historian, making her the first woman in Arizona to hold public office. She also founded a museum to preserve the history of Arizona.

Angela Hammer See page 61.

Emil Haury See page 28.

Carl Trumbull Hayden (1877–1972) was an influential politician who served in Congress for 56 years, 42 of them in the U.S. Senate. He was born in Hayden's Ferry (now Tempe).

David Henrie (1989–) is an actor and television writer best known for his roles on *How I Met Your Mother*, *Wizards of Waverly Place*, and *That's So Raven*. Born in California, he grew up in Phoenix.

Reggie Jackson See page 84.

Helen Hull Jacobs (1908–1997) was one of the world's top 10 tennis players from 1932 to 1940. She was born in Globe.

Waylon Jennings (1937–2002) was a country music singer-songwriter and musician. He also appeared in numerous movies and TV shows. Born in Texas, he worked and lived in Arizona for many years.

Viola Jimulla (1878–1966) served as the Yavapai chief for 26 years. During this time, she helped establish the Prescott Yavapai Tribal Council.

Eusebio Kino See page 42.

Elisabeth Kübler-Ross (1926–2004) was born in Switzerland and was a long-time resident of Scottsdale. Her groundbreaking book *On Death and Dying* describes five stages that people go through as they face their own deaths. Ross also taught psychiatry at the University of Colorado and the University of Chicago.

Percival Lawrence Lowell (1855–1916) was an astronomer and founder of the Lowell Observatory in Flagstaff, one of the United States' oldest observatories. He is best known for his work that led to the discovery of Pluto after his death. The name Pluto is based on his initials, PL.

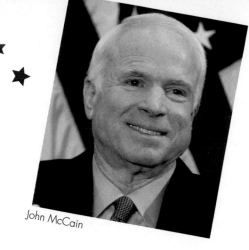

John McCain

John McCain (1936–) is a longtime U.S. senator from Arizona. He served in the U.S. Navy during the Vietnam War. His plane was shot down, and he was held captive for more than five years. In 2008, he became the Republican candidate for the presidency.

Stephenie Meyer See page 83.

Phil Mickelson (1970–), one of the world's top golfers, played golf at Arizona State University before turning pro. He was born in California and spent much of his youth in Arizona.

Charles Mingus See page 81.

Arturo Moreno See page 105.

Nampeyo See page 32.

Nampeyo

Janet Napolitano (1957–) served as the Arizona attorney general before being elected governor of Arizona two times.

Joy Navasie (1919–) is a Hopi potter who uses traditional methods to create exquisite white pots with black and red decorations. She is sometimes called Frog Woman because she uses a frog as her symbol on the pots she makes.

Lorena Ochoa (1981–) is a professional golfer from Mexico who plays on the U.S.-based LPGA tour. A former student at the University of Arizona, she is the first Mexican golfer to be ranked number one.

Sandra Day O'Connor See page 93.

Lori Piestewa See page 67.

Charles Poston (1825–1902) represented Arizona Territory in Congress. Because of his efforts to have Arizona declared a territory separate from New Mexico, he is sometimes called the Father of Arizona.

Geneva Ramon See page 79.

William Rehnquist (1924–2005) served on the U.S. Supreme Court for 34 years, 19 of them as chief justice. He worked as a lawyer in Phoenix before becoming a judge.

Linda Ronstadt

Linda Ronstadt (1946–), a native of Tucson, is a singer known for her wide vocal range. She sang with the Stone Poneys in the late 1960s before breaking out on her own. She is of Mexican descent and has produced a few albums of Mexican songs, including *Canciones de Mi Padre* (*Songs of My Father*).

Garry Shandling (1949–) is a comedian who grew up in Tucson. He starred in the TV series *The Larry Sanders Show* and *It's Garry Shandling's Show.*

Leslie Marmon Silko (1948–) is a novelist who mixes traditional Native American tales into her stories of modern Native Americans. She lives in Tucson.

Karsten Solheim (1911–2000) was a designer who created PING golf clubs. He grew up in Norway but founded his golf club business in Phoenix.

David Spade (1964–) is a comedian and actor who has appeared on TV shows such as *Saturday Night Live* and *Just Shoot Me!* He was born in Michigan but grew up in Scottsdale.

Jordin Sparks (1989–) is a singer who was voted the winner of *American Idol* in 2007. She was born in Phoenix.

Jordin Sparks

Emma Stone

Steven Spielberg (1946–), one of the most popular film directors in history, grew up in Phoenix. He has made blockbusters such as *Raiders of the Lost Ark* and *E.T.: The Extra-Terrestrial.*

Emma Stone (1988–), born in Scottsdale, has starred in major motion pictures, including *Easy A* and *Crazy, Stupid, Love.* She also starred as Gwen Stacy in *The Amazing Spider-Man.*

Louis Tewanima (1879–1969) was a Hopi runner who won a silver medal at the 1912 Olympics. He held the American record in the 10,000-meter race for 52 years.

Pat Tillman (1976–2004) left his professional football career playing for the Arizona Cardinals to join the U.S. Army in the wake of the September 11, 2001, terrorist attacks. He was killed while serving in Afghanistan. Tillman had also been a star linebacker at Arizona State University, where he also earned many academic awards.

Morris Udall (1922–1998) served as a U.S. representative from Arizona from 1961 to 1991. A former professional basketball player, he was known for his liberal political views. In 1976, he ran unsuccessfully for the Democratic Party nomination for president, losing to Jimmy Carter, who won the presidency later that year.

Annie Dodge Wauneka See page 96.

Dot Wilkinson (1921–) is a member of the Hall of Fame for two different sports: softball and bowling. She played softball from 1933 to 1965, winning three national titles and being selected as an all-American amateur softball player 19 times. She won the Women's International Bowling Queens Tournament in 1962 and the Women's International Bowling Congress singles in 1963.

Frank Lloyd Wright (1867–1959) was one of the most innovative architects of the 20th century. He was born in Wisconsin, but later in life he built Taliesin, his home and studio near Phoenix. The Guggenheim Museum in New York City is one of his many designs.

Frank Lloyd Wright

RESOURCES

★ ★ ★

BOOKS

Nonfiction

Augustin, Byron, and Jake Kubena. *The Grand Canyon.* New York: Marshall Cavendish Benchmark, 2010.

Cunningham, Kevin, and Peter Benoit. *The Pueblo.* New York: Children's Press, 2011.

Hartz, George. *Arizona's National Parks and Monuments.* Charleston, S.C., 2013.

Lyon, Robin. *The Spanish Missions of Arizona.* New York: Children's Press, 2010.

Miller, Heather. *The Hoover Dam.* Chicago: Norwood House Press, 2014.

Sullivan, George. *Geronimo: Apache Renegade.* New York: Sterling, 2010.

Turner, Jim. *Arizona: A Celebration of the Grand Canyon State.* Layton, Utah: Gibbs Smith, 2011.

Woog, Adam. *Wyatt Earp.* Chelsea House, 2010.

Fiction

Bruchac, Joseph. *Code Talker: A Novel About the Navajo Marines of World War Two.* New York: Dial, 2005.

Burks, Brian. *Runs With Horses.* Minneapolis: Tandem Library, 1999.

Momaday, Natachee Scott. *Owl in the Cedar Tree.* Lincoln: University of Nebraska Press, 1992.

O'Dell, Scott. *Sing Down the Moon.* New York: Laurel-Leaf, 1997.

Ostrom, Laura. *The Fried-Egg Quilt: A Pioneer Journey to Arizona Territory.* Lincoln, Neb.: iUniverse, Inc., 2004.

Price, Joan. *Truth Is a Bright Star: A Hopi Adventure.* Berkeley, Calif.: Tricycle Press, 2001.

Visit this Scholastic Web site for more information on Arizona:
www.factsfornow.scholastic.com
Enter the keyword **Arizona**

INDEX

★ ★ ★

AUTHOR'S TIPS AND SOURCE NOTES

★　★　★

To research this book, I asked the resource librarian at my local library to help gather materials. The books soon came pouring in. Two useful books that are also interesting and fun are *Weird Arizona: Your Travel Guide to Arizona's Local Legends and Best Kept Secrets* by Wesley Treat and *The Great Arizona Almanac: Facts About Arizona* by Dean Smith. For outdoor life, *Arizona Wildlife Viewing Guide* by Sharen Adams and Sharon Mallman proved very useful.